EXTREMISM

The MIT Press Essential Knowledge Series

EXTREMISM

J. M. BERGER

The MIT Press | Cambridge, Massachusetts | London, England

This book was set in Chaparral Pro by Toppan Best-set Premedia Limited. Printed and bound in the United States of America.

Library of Congress Cataloging-in-Publication Data

Names: Berger, J. M. (John M.), 1967- author.
Title: Extremism / J. M. Berger.
Description: Cambridge, MA : The MIT Press, 2018. | Series: The MIT press essential knowledge series | Includes bibliographical references and index.
Identifiers: LCCN 2018007483 | ISBN 9780262535878 (pbk. : alk. paper)
Subjects: LCSH: Radicalism. | Political violence.
Classification: LCC HN49.R33 B464 2018 | DDC 303.48/4--dc23 LC record available at https://lccn.loc.gov/2018007483

10   9   8   7   6   5   4   3   2

CONTENTS

SERIES FOREWORD

The MIT Press Essential Knowledge series offers accessible, concise, beautifully produced pocket-size books on topics of current interest. Written by leading thinkers, the books in this series deliver expert overviews of subjects that range from the cultural and the historical to the scientific and the technical.

In today's era of instant information gratification, we have ready access to opinions, rationalizations, and superficial descriptions. Much harder to come by is the foundational knowledge that informs a principled understanding of the world. Essential Knowledge books fill that need. Synthesizing specialized subject matter for nonspecialists and engaging critical topics through fundamentals, each of these compact volumes offers readers a point of access to complex ideas.

Bruce Tidor
Professor of Biological Engineering and Computer Science
Massachusetts Institute of Technology

ACKNOWLEDGMENTS

As always, I am deeply indebted to many people who helped me along the way to this book. Most of the concepts discussed herein were developed with support and guidance from Alastair Reed, head of the Counter-Terrorism Strategic Communications Project. I am grateful for his friendship and support.

The work of Haroro J. Ingram, published through the International Centre for Counter-Terrorism—The Hague and the CTSC Project, was deeply influential on my own. I benefited greatly from our conversations and his feedback in general and on this manuscript. The direction of this work also was shaped by his critical contributions regarding messaging broadly and his development of crucial elements of theory regarding crisis and solution constructs. His publications, cited in the bibliography, are highly recommended as a companion to this book. The work of Michael Hogg on uncertainty and extremism, and the work of others building on his concepts, also influenced on this work in very important ways.

This book came about after I gave a lecture at a conference at the Paris Institute for Advanced Study (Paris IAS), where I met MIT Press editor Matthew Browne. Thanks are due to Itzhak Fried, who organized that fascinating event, and Jessica Stern, my friend and past collaborator, who brokered my invitation and whose support in general has opened many doors for me. Thanks also to Anne-Marie Bono of the MIT Press, for guiding the process of publication and to my agent, Martha Kaplan. Thanks also to Maura Conway and Lisa McInerney of VOX-Pol for their support of this book and other generosities.

Finally, and most of all, this book and all my work in this field, and pretty much all of the good things in my life in general, would not be possible without the love and support I have received from my wife, Janet.

DELENDA EST

In a 1964 U.S. Supreme Court opinion attempting to define pornography for legal purposes, Justice Potter Stewart summed up the nebulous nature of the concept in seven now-infamous words. He couldn't offer a workable definition, he wrote, but "I know it when I see it."[1]

More than fifty years later, we find this test applied to one of the world's most pressing problems, a rising tide of extremist movements that are destabilizing civil societies around the globe. Virtually everyone acknowledges the severity of the threat, but extremism is still most often classified according to Stewart's criteria: we know it when we see it. And as with pornography, we do not all agree about what passes the test.

The dictionary definition is circular: *extremism* is "the quality or state of being extreme" or "the advocacy of extreme measures or views."[2] In academia and policy circles, widely varying definitions have been proffered. Some are simplistic,[3] and others are frustratingly elaborate.[4] Many are specialized to one particular type of movement, such as jihadist terrorism.[5] Some are predicated on the use of violence.[6] Often, scholars define *extremism* relative to the "center" or "norms" of any given society.[7] In politics, extremism is an increasingly convenient insult—a way to characterize and condemn what "the other guys" believe.

The flaws in these definitions should be apparent. A circular definition ("extremists are extreme") is meaningless and highly vulnerable to abuse because it can apply to anyone whose views you disagree with. A definition that specifies a religious dimension excludes secular movements and vice versa. A definition predicated on violence excludes a world of movements that "we know when we see them," such as some segregationists, the alt-right, and at least some branches of the Muslim Brotherhood. A definition based on the norms or "center" of a society is especially perilous because it excludes successful and important historical extremist regimes, such as institutionalized racial slavery in America and Nazi Germany.

The answer to the question "What is extremism?" seems like it should be obvious, but it definitely isn't. And in a world where violent extremism is widely acknowledged as a defining challenge of our age, that failure of definition has huge real-world consequences.

In a world where violent extremism is widely acknowledged as a defining challenge of our age, that failure of definition has huge real-world consequences.

In the United States, the term *extremist* is frequently hurled, shorn of context, across racial and partisan divides. Many in the wider West contend that the entire religion of Islam is inherently extreme, arguing for policies that range from the curtailment of civil rights to mass internment. Within Islam itself, furious debates rage about which sect, movement, or nation is normative and which is extremist.

These debates influence the study of extremism. There are perhaps three times as many academic studies referencing jihadism as there are referencing white nationalism.[8] Pseudo-intellectuals, some in positions of political power, have argued that white nationalism is far less important than jihadism, despite the fact that white nationalism has a far longer and more deadly history. And they have shaped policies accordingly.[9]

If you believe that only "the other guys" can produce extremists and that your own identity group cannot, you may be an extremist yourself. History provides ample evidence that extremism is part of the human condition and not the exclusive province of any single race, religion, or nation. Not all violence is extremism, nor are all of humanity's countless wars, conflicts, and atrocities. Many cases are ambiguous, but some clearly align with our modern understanding of the word.

The diversity and ubiquity of the problem can be seen in a review of historical outbreaks of significant violence driven by ideological belief. The examples that follow were selected based in significant part on the author's previous study, which has followed the availability of translated texts describing articulated ideologies. There are many more relevant cases from all parts of the world, and this chapter should be understood as illustrative rather than comprehensive. Some readers may take issue with some of the examples cited in this chapter. To a certain extent, that's the point of this exercise. But the chapters that follow offer a definition of extremism that transcends the cultural norms of a given moment in history.

As you read this brief tour through history, consider some of the following questions: Is extremism concerned with the supremacy of one's own group, or is it defined by hatred of the "other"? Do extremists emerge on the scene suddenly, or do they evolve from mainstream movements? Are they found only on the margins of society? Is violence a necessary component of extremism? How do extremists decide on their beliefs? Are they rational? How can we define extremism objectively when so many possible variations exist?

The First Extremists?

While the annals of the ancient world are full of violence, the social context and ideological justifications that survive are often incomplete. One of the earliest examples of a social trend that resembles extremism as we know it today can be found in the Roman war on Carthage in the second century BCE, which has been described by Yale scholar Ben Kiernan as "the first genocide."[10]

Carthage, located in modern-day Tunisia, was the capital of one of ancient Rome's regional competitors. After three devastating wars, Rome captured the city and disarmed the citizenry. Yet some Roman politicians argued that the threat posed by Carthage was so dire that it could not be addressed simply by conquest.

A Roman senator known as Cato the Elder was famously reported to conclude every speech he gave to the Senate with the phrase "Carthago delenda est" ("Carthage must be destroyed"), no matter what the subject of the speech happened to be. Cato was an early populist-nationalist. He was a paleo-conservative even relative to the standards of the day—militaristic, misogynistic, and racist,[11] comparing the perceived decadence of his contemporaneous society to a mythical golden age of days past. He believed that Carthage represented a threat to the existence of Rome and the purity of its culture. Because of this, victory was not enough: "Carthago delenda est."

The Third Punic War began with Carthage almost immediately surrendering to Rome and disarming. Unsatisfied with the terms of that surrender, Rome demanded that the Carthaginians abandon the city, which the Senate had already decided to destroy. When the residents refused to leave, Rome launched a siege that ended with Carthage razed to the ground. The decision to continue past the Carthaginian surrender and the rhetoric of Cato frame the destruction of Carthage squarely as a recognizable example of extremism. It is estimated that 150,000 or more died when the city fell.[12]

Carthage is arguably the earliest well-documented historical example of genocide and nationalist violent extremism. There are reports of more ancient events—such as the Trojan War or scriptural accounts that purport to describe Israel's extermination of the Amelekites. Although these events are not as well documented as the destruction of Carthage, they suggest that a concept of extremism likely existed even earlier in history.[13]

After Carthage, historical records became more robust, and other examples quickly emerged. One identity movement founded during the early first century CE was known as the Zealots. Much has been written about the sect, although some of that scholarship is colored by Christian interpretations of the group.[14]

One of many anti-Roman groups, the Zealots asserted a unique Jewish identity for occupied Judea and condemned both the Roman invaders and the Jews who cooperated in governing under Roman rule. Its founder condemned Jewish collaborators as cowards and appeared to endorse a theocratic government ruled by priests or a priest-king. Adherents also believed in "zeal," the root of the movement's name, meaning a militant enforcement of its views through violence. They battled the provisional government in Jerusalem.[15]

A group within or related to the Zealots, the Sicarii, were said to go further, believing "there should be no lordship of man over man, that God is the only ruler" and killing a Jewish high priest in 65 CE for acceding to Roman rule. The Sicarii were known for carrying out assassinations, property destruction, and theft. According to Josephus, a Jewish-born Roman historian, they "mingled themselves among the multitude, and concealed daggers under their garments," attacking without warning to strike terror in both Roman and Jewish targets. They became known as perpetrators of atrocities. According to Josephus, the Sicarii committed mass suicide rather than surrender to a siege on their mountain redoubt of Masada in 74 CE,[16] although historians have many questions about the veracity of this account.[17]

The Dark and Middle Ages

In 657 CE, the then-young religion of Islam experienced one of its first major schisms with the rebellion of a sect known to its enemies the Kharijites or Khawarij (from the Arabic word for *seceding*).[18] Adherents referred to themselves as As-Shurah, or "the sellers," in reference to a Quranic verse about selling life in the temporal world in exchange for eternal life in paradise.[19]

The Kharijites broke with the Islamic caliphate in a dispute over succession. The movement was concerned with restoring the practice of Islam as they imagined it to have been two generations previously. The caliph of the day, Ali, brutally crushed the Kharijite rebellion and was subsequently assassinated by one of the sect's adherents.

As with many historical movements, views of the Kharijites are colored by the passage of time and the well-known effect of history being written by the victors. For instance, Irenaeus, one of the Fathers of the Church, was for many years the primary authority on the Gnostic sect of early Christianity. But the discovery of a cache of well-preserved original Gnostic texts in 1945 revealed that his descriptions of the sect were often and significantly inaccurate.[20] Histories of heresy are written by the orthodox victors.[21]

Thus, the Kharijites have become associated with violent extremism thanks to the work of mainstream Islamic historians over many years, but it is not entirely clear how much of its reputation is grounded in reality. Nelly Lahoud, a scholar of political Islam, writes that the notoriety of the Kharijites grew in direct proportion to the fame and status of Ali. Additionally, Muslim scholars have in recent years come to rely on the term as a pejorative to condemn jihadist terrorism, further coloring views of the group.[22]

With that caveat in place, the understanding of the Kharijites as extremists may have some basis. Like the Zealots, the Kharijites are remembered for their zeal, both in their stringent practice of Islam and the use of political violence in its defense. Most accounts agree that they were hardcore fundamentalists looking back to a golden age of Islam, albeit one that had barely passed in their lifetimes. Their commitment was so focused that it was said they could seduce even their enemies to become adherents.

Kharijites were said to evaluate other Muslims for purity and correct belief, killing those who failed to meet their definition of Islam. They were reputed to have brutally killed Muslims who failed the test, along with their families, including women and fetuses cut from the womb.[23] They may have believed that any sin rendered the sinner an apostate from Islam.[24]

The wars between (and within) Christianity and Islam during the Middle Ages are too vast to explore in detail here. But one particularly memorable case of heresy-hunting took place in the thirteenth century Roman Catholic Church. The Cathars were a Christian religious sect based in the south of France whose beliefs were wildly different from the orthodoxy of Rome. Its practices were also notably different, with unique sacraments and a commitment to living modestly, in contrast to some Catholic clerics of the day.

A succession of popes sent emissaries and messages to urge repentance in increasingly dire terms. Some of these entreaties reportedly met with violent responses. Finally, Pope Innocent III called a crusade, offering the forgiveness of all sins for those who would "tear up the unserviceable roots from the vineyard of the Lord" and calling on Christian men "kindled with the zeal of orthodox faith to avenge just blood—which does not cease to cry out from earth to heaven, until the Lord of Vengeance shall descend from heaven to earth to confound both subverted and subvertors."[25]

The toll was staggering, resulting in widespread torture and the massacre of likely hundreds of thousands of Cathars until the religion and its supporters had been eradicated. The conflict between the Catholic Church and the Cathars also led directly to the establishment of one of the most horrific institutions in history, the Inquisition.[26]

The New World

Starting in the sixteenth century, Spanish conquistadors sought to colonize the Americas through a program that may have started as military conquest but soon escalated into racial extremism. They perpetrated the most horrific genocide in human history, resulting in the extermination of whole societies of indigenous peoples in the Americas. The actions of the conquistadors left as many as 70 million dead through a combination of intentional massacres, the effects of enslavement, and the introduction of deadly diseases.[27]

The line between war and extremism is often muddy, but the conquistadors executed their campaign in reprehensible excess and with the support of a legitimizing ideology. Spanish philosopher Juan Ginés de Sepúlveda wrote that the indigenous people of the Americas were "half-men" or "homunculi," who possessed "barely the vestiges of humanity" and deserved only conquest and enslavement.[28] Later colonizers of the New World and Australia also relied on various ideological justifications for their acts, although these were often a thinly veiled excuse to indulge a cruel and epic greed.[29]

Slavery, broadly, had been a part of warfare and conquest for millennia, as well as being a criminal punishment or a mandated satisfaction of debt in some cultures. Hereditary or chattel slavery—the concept that a slave's descendants must also be slaves—was less common, but it became a growing force after the fifteenth century as a series of papal proclamations helped legitimize the practice in conjunction with the colonization of the Americas and the concurrent rise of the African slave trade. During the course of these debates, a variety of conflicting religious views (both Catholic and Protestant) emerged as to whether indigenous peoples and other nonwhite races could be considered human and whether their enslavement was justified regardless. The institution—and its racialization—grew despite these ambiguities and shifting views.[30]

In the colonial Americas, Virginia passed a law legalizing hereditary slavery, and other colonies soon followed, embedding the practice deeply in the economy and culture of the nascent United States. Disagreements over the morality of slavery slowly grew into a force strong enough to break a nation. The rise of the abolitionist movement in the early nineteenth century and its attacks on the legitimacy of what was called the "peculiar institution" led to the crystallization and codification of extremist proslavery ideologies.[31]

"Can these two distinct races of people now living together as master and servant, be ever separated?" asked the proslavery writer Thomas Roderick Dew. "Can the black be sent back to his African home, or will the day ever arrive when he can be liberated from his thralldom, and mount upwards in the scale of civilization and rights, to an equality with the white?"[32]

In order to preserve slavery, extensive ideological justifications were advanced. Southern intellectuals leapt to the task, citing sources both biblical and "scientific." They also drew on historical precedent, citing past civilizations that had thrived on the institution (often eliding the distinction between nonhereditary slavery and its heredi-tary, racialized offshoot).[33]

No one really knows how many slaves were held in cap-tivity in the United States and elsewhere over the duration of the practice. Likely a minimum of 10 million African slaves were trafficked to the Americas, and at the conclu-sion of the Civil War, nearly 4 million slaves were freed in the United States alone. The total human cost of the African slave trade and the succeeding generations of he-reditary slavery certainly run into the tens of millions, one of the gravest shames in the history of humanity and one of extremism's greatest triumphs.[34]

The Twentieth Century and Beyond

The origins of anti-Semitic extremism, in its religious aspect, can be traced back millennia (see chapter 3), but in France and Germany during the late nineteenth century, it evolved into an ideology that viewed Jewish identity not just as religious but also as racial. Anti-Semitic beliefs took hold with special ferocity in Germany, where decades of war and social upheaval created conditions ideal for the persecution of a minority that could blamed for loss and uncertainty.[35]

A confluence of events, anchored by German nation-alism and virulent anti-Semitism, led ultimately to the depredations of the Nazi regime, which killed 6 million

Jews and at least 12 million others between 1933 and 1945 through campaigns of genocide, the horrors of concentration camps, programs of mass starvation, and other atrocities outside of the wartime death toll, which added tens of millions more on all sides.[36]

Even in defeat, elements of the poisonous Nazi ideology live on today in hundreds of successor movements around the world that are dedicated not just to German racial purity and nationalism but to a broad spectrum of white supremacist beliefs, from the United States to Greece, Russia to Australia. The influence of Nazism endures today not only among relatively small groups of direct adherents but in broader international and political dynamics,[37] including a host of politically corrosive conspiracists who endlessly recycle anti-Semitic tropes using euphemisms such as "globalist."[38]

The twentieth century was rife with extremism—the anarchist assassination of U.S. President William McKinley in 1901, the Serbian nationalist assassination of Austrian Archduke Franz Ferdinand in 1914 (one of the events that helped trigger World War I), the Stalinist massacres of the 1930s, and the slaughter of as many as a million Tutsis in Rwanda in 1994.[39] There have been many more—too many to describe fully in a single chapter or even a single volume.

In the winter of 1979, a series of events rocked the Muslim world, setting the stage for the extremist scourge that dominates most discussion of the topic today—the jihadist movement. Iranian revolutionaries overthrew their nation's secular government and established an extreme theocracy, setting the stage for the later emergence of the formidable Shia jihadist movement Hezbollah and a host of other Shia sectarian militias. Soon after, in Saudi Arabia, a band of apocalyptic extremists laid siege to the Grand Mosque in Mecca, the holiest site in Islam, in a terrorist attack that left hundreds dead and paralyzed the country for weeks.

Perhaps most fatefully, the Soviet Union invaded Afghanistan at the end of 1979, triggering a decades-long sequence of events that has shaped much of the twenty-first century. In response to the invasion of a Muslim country, hundreds and then thousands of foreign fighters made their way to Afghanistan to fight the Soviets as mujahideen, warriors in defense of their coreligionists. In the United States, the mujahideen were seen at first as freedom fighters. Their leaders were invited to the United States to meet with American politicians. They received overt praise from the State Department and covert support from the Central Intelligence Agency. The head of the foreign fighter battalions, Abdullah Azzam, traveled to the United States repeatedly, openly recruiting American Muslims to join the battle.[40]

As the nearly decade-long war began to wind down with the Soviets in retreat, veterans of the foreign fighter movement decided their work was not finished. In 1988, Osama bin Laden organized a small group of Afghanistan veterans into al Qaeda, an organization dedicated to reshaping the Muslim world. Al Qaeda began as a small and secretive cabal lending aid to Muslim terrorist and insurgent groups around the globe.

During the 1990s, Serbian nationalist extremists carried out genocidal attacks that resulted in thousands of Bosnian Muslims being killed, displaced, and placed in concentration camps. These extremist attacks provoked an extremist response. At least hundreds of foreign jihadist extremists—many trained by or affiliated with al Qaeda—joined the Muslim defense effort, alongside hundreds more jihadists of Bosnian origin.[41] Although an uneasy peace was brokered between the warring sides in 1995, extremists from both camps continue to plague the region in significant numbers.[42]

Al Qaeda sought to overthrow corrupt Middle Eastern regimes and replace them with Sunni theocracies. Because bin Laden and his cohort believed the movement could not accomplish this without depriving Arab rulers of American financial and military support, al Qaeda began to direct terrorist attacks against the United States, first by supporting loosely connected extremist groups (as in the 1993 World Trade Center bombing) and later with its own highly professional operations (such as the 1998 synchronized bombings of U.S. embassies in East Africa).

On September 11, 2001, al Qaeda carried out the most devastating terrorist attack in history, hijacking four airplanes and successfully crashing three of them into the World Trade Center towers and the Pentagon. In response, the United States launched a "War on Terror" that continues to this day. The resulting social and political upheaval has too often placed Muslims at the center of public debate and policy regarding extremism.[43]

In the wake of the U.S. invasion of Afghanistan, where al Qaeda was based, the organization spread out geographically, first under a relatively centralized affiliate model. But over time, the cohesion of the organization was tested by internal politics and external pressures. The affiliates increasingly waged insurgencies in their local realms and neglected their original focus on the United States and a global jihad.

The most important fracture took place in Iraq, home to the first official al Qaeda affiliate, which formed in response to the 2003 U.S. invasion of that country. Al Qaeda in Iraq was founded by Abu Musab al-Zarqawi, a Jordanian jihadist whose views were even more extreme than those of bin Laden. Al Qaeda in Iraq almost immediately came into conflict with its parent group. After a decade fighting U.S. and Iraqi forces with varying degrees of success, it went through a series of reorganizations and finally established itself as an entity completely independent of al Qaeda, known as the Islamic State or ISIS.

The Islamic State, which is discussed at length in the chapters that follow, represented an evolution of al Qaeda's ideology. It was more violent and against a much wider variety of targets. Where al Qaeda tried (selectively and with mixed results) to minimize Sunni Muslim casualties in its attacks, Islamic State massacred Sunnis by the hundreds. Where al Qaeda put less emphasis on the divide between the Sunni and Shia sects of Islam, Islamic State calculated its attacks to widen it, making Shia Muslims its archenemy, above all others, even the hated Americans and Jews.[44]

As jihadist movements proliferated and diversified, the issue of understanding extremism became more contentious, contested, and confusing. In Syria, Bashar al-Assad's regime brutally slaughters civilians by the thousands and justifies the carnage by claiming it is fighting extremists.[45] Within the Syrian opposition itself, fractious infighting revolves around the question of which rebels are the noble opposition and which are jihadist extremists.[46] And even the true jihadists in Syria are splintered into more and less radical camps, constantly accusing each other of extremism while exonerating themselves.[47] Jihadist rebels define their extremism against each other and against Islamic State, which is a deadly enemy to most of them, despite great similarities in their ideologies.[48]

The complexity of extremism now bedevils all discussions, exacerbated by an all-too-human tendency to describe any political difference in the extremist frame. Reasonable critiques of Israeli policies toward Palestinians sometimes veer into anti-Semitic tropes. Meanwhile, an internationally designated terrorist group, Hamas, controls significant swaths of Palestinian territories, participating in governance even while splitting internally into more and less extreme factions.[49]

The rising alt-right movement in the United States predicates bigotry against Muslims on the assertion that Islam itself is fundamentally extremist, and the high frequency of terrorist attacks by Islamic State throws fuel on that fire. In the view of the alt-right, every Muslim is a potential terrorist and an active cultural infiltrator seeking to establish Islamic religious rule in the United States.[50]

In Myanmar, Buddhists have been swept up in this cycle, practicing discrimination or worse against members of its Muslim Rohingya minority for decades before opening a new campaign of ethnic cleansing that is tilting rapidly toward genocide at the time of this writing. Like anti-Muslim extremists in other countries, radical Buddhist monk Ashin Wirathu says his victims are the real extremists. "You can be full of kindness and love, but you cannot sleep next to a mad dog," Wirathu has said, seeking to reconcile traditional Buddhist teaching with his campaign of hate and fearmongering.[51]

If there is any lesson to learn from these modern and historical examples, it is this: defining extremism is not

The complexity of extremism now bedevils all discussions, exacerbated by an all-too-human tendency to describe any political difference in the extremist frame.

a casual matter. "I know it when I see it" is not an acceptable standard when lives are at stake. It is not enough for a world where the course of history has repeatedly changed as a result of extremist violence.

So how do we begin? How can we understand extremism outside of the realm of a single ideological strain? How can we separate our conversations about extremism from ordinary political disagreements? How can a better understanding of extremism reduce its terrible cost in human lives? This book attempts to answer these questions.

WHAT IS EXTREMISM?

Famed political theorist Hannah Arendt argued ideologies were modern inventions that began to manifest a significant political impact only with the arrival of figures like Adolf Hitler and Josef Stalin.[1] But that assertion (made in the context of totalitarianism) is belied by the history reviewed in the previous chapter. While far from complete, this review of identifiably extremist belief illustrates the daunting scope of a problem that has plagued humanity since almost the beginning of recorded history.

The objective study of extremism leads quickly to three crucial truths:

- Extremism is rarely simple.

- Extremism is not the province of any single race, religion, or political school.

- Extremism can be profoundly consequential in societies.

These stipulations open us up to a world of trouble. How do we begin to approach a challenge that is so diverse? Can we reasonably hope to defeat a problem that has endured throughout most of human history? And what is extremism, anyway?

Despite their diversity, extremist movements have common elements that provide a path to understanding. One of the most useful frames for discussing extremism is known as social identity theory, an approach to understanding intergroup dynamics pioneered by social psychologists Henri Tajfel and John C. Turner.[2]

Social identity theory stipulates that people categorize themselves and others as members of competing social groups. The **in-group** is a group of people who share an identity, such as religious, racial, or national. It is the group to which one belongs—the "us" in "us versus them." The **out-group** is a group of people who are excluded from a specific in-group. They are part of "them."

In this book, in-groups and out-groups each represent an **identity**—a set of qualities that are understood to make a person or group distinct from other persons or groups. People who share a common identity may form an **identity collective**, a group of people who are defined by nation, religion, race, or some other shared trait, interest or concern.

The *in* in *in-group* does not denote dominance, popularity, or a value judgment. In and out are relative statuses.

My in-group may be your out-group, and my out-group may be your in-group. For any given identity, you are either in the group or out of it.

For most social movements, in-groups and out-groups are simply different, which is not and should not be a reflexive reason for hostility. Pluralistic societies accept and even celebrate differences between individuals and groups. Still, people have a natural tendency to admire and esteem their own in-groups in comparison to any out-group. For extremist movements, this tendency is vastly amplified. Loyalty to the in-group is all important, and certain out-groups are perceived as menacing enemies.

Identifying in-groups and out-groups is not a purely binary process. As we will see, an in-group is not always unitary, and it can be subdivided in meaningful ways. An in-group can also have more than one out-group. For instance, Sunni jihadists designate many different out-groups as part of an overlapping circle of enemies. Many white nationalists believe that each race has distinct qualities and represents a different kind of threat to their in-group. In such circumstances, extremists may prescribe different tactics for dealing with different out-groups.

In-groups and out-groups are not always obvious. They have to be defined. **Categorization** is the act of understanding yourself to be part of an in-group and determining whether others are part of your in-group or your out-group. **Social identification** is an act of self-categorization in which an individual decides that he or she is part of an in-group. Categorization has psychological consequences that shape how people and groups view themselves and others, which are discussed in the pages that follow.

Often, in-groups are perceived to have more legitimacy than out-groups. In this context, **legitimacy** can be defined as the belief that an identity collective has a right to exist and may be rightfully defined, maintained, and protected. The word has many dimensions in everyday use, most of which are not relevant to extremism. As we shall see, the quest for legitimacy is a key element in many extremist movements.

All extremist groups (and many nonextremist groups) have some sort of ideology. As with the word *extremist*, there are many definitions of ideology, and some are quite complex. These more expansive definitions may be necessary to encompass nonextremist political and religious groups.[3] In the context of this book, however, an **extremist ideology** is a collection of texts that describe who is part of the in-group, who is part of an out-group, and how the in-group should interact with the out-group. Ideological texts can include a wide range of media types, including books, images, lectures, videos, and even conversations.

Many scholars prefer to define *ideology* chiefly in terms of ideas and concepts.[4] I find this unnecessarily amorphous. Ideas and concepts are contained in texts, and a movement cannot adopt an ideology unless and until it

The quest for legitimacy is a key element in many extremist movements.

is transmitted in a text. Without transmission and narrative, there would be no extremist groups, only individual extremists separately following their own self-designed beliefs. In addition to highlighting the importance of transmission, a focus on texts makes it easier to systematically analyze the contents of an ideology and track its evolution over time.

A Bestiary of Extremists

The first chapter of this book provides anecdotal examples of the diversity of extremist movements, drawn from history in a roughly chronological order. This section attempts to organize these examples into categories for the most common and consequential types of extremism. Some extremist movements are a hybrid of the categories listed below, and others are highly particularized subsets.

Not all violence is extremist, and not all extremists are violent. Many crimes and wars involve violence to promote or protect individual or group interests, such as profit or legitimate self-defense. While extremist sentiments often overlap with crime and war, the mere act of violence— even horrific, evil violence—is not inherently extremist.

This can lead to some murky and unclear situations that require significant unpacking, and some questions may never be cleanly resolved. For instance, ethnicity plays a significant role in the Mafia and other ethnic criminal gangs, but promotion of that ethnic identity is often secondary to other considerations, such as profit.

Similar ambiguities pertain to hate crimes, discussed in more detail in chapter 4. Some hate crimes are clearly driven by extremist ideologies (for example, an attack by a group of neo-Nazi skinheads on an African American). But others may be examples of what I call "pedestrian" hate—the simple dislike of people who are different.

An example might be a drunken heterosexual man attacking a gay man in a bar, motivated by fear, anger, or simple bigotry. The attacker may not rely on an articulated ideological belief to justify his violence. The lack of ideology does not lessen the seriousness of such attacks, but it does raise questions about whether all hate crimes should be considered extremism. My own inclination is to classify pedestrian hate as distinct from ideological extremism, but there is plenty of room for debate. For instance, the attacker's attitude may have its roots in an ideological concept that has been widely diffused in society, obscuring its origins. Government data on hate crimes is often deficient with respect to detailed motives and potential ideological influences, and focused study might help clarify this question.

Relatedly, terrorism must be disentangled from extremism. Although they often travel in tandem, the two are not the same thing. Terrorism is a tactic, whereas extremism is a belief system. Because extremist movements are often small, they are motivated to adopt asymmetric tactics such as terrorism. When extremists do use terrorism, they usually create ideological justifications to support that decision. But many extremists eschew terrorism, and not everyone who employs the tactic of terrorism is necessarily an extremist.

The major categories of extremism include racial/ethnic, religious, nationalist, anti-government, anarchist, classist, single-issue movements, and gender, sexual orientation, and sexual identity. These categories often overlap, sometimes in self-reinforcing ways, such as the pairing of a religion with a national identity, or the adoption of antigovernment tenets by racists. At times, such fused ideologies can be more complex and toxic than the sum of their parts.

Racial/Ethnic

Racial extremist movements promote a racial or ethnic in-group and call for hostile acts targeting one or more racial or ethnic out-groups. *Race* is sometimes used as a synonym for ethnicity. At other times, race is a socially constructed concept that incorporates ethnic distinctions. The most obvious example of the latter is the distinction between white and black. Each of these terms has been defined in different ways at different times. For instance,

Terrorism is a tactic, whereas extremism is a belief system.

Polish, Irish, and Italian immigrants to the United States are now considered white but were not always.[5]

Racial extremism is one of the most intractable problems in the world. Unlike other forms of extremism, such as those based on religious or political identities, someone who has been assigned to a racial out-group generally cannot opt to join the in-group in order to escape persecution.

Members of the in-group are the sole authority in determining who belongs to the out-group, and they spend considerable intellectual capital in trying to create impassable boundaries between the "races." Perhaps most infamously, the Nazis crafted detailed laws defining who could be considered German (and therefore entitled to the privileges of citizenship) and who was a Jew (and therefore subject to persecution). They criminalized intermarriage in order to prevent Jews from "becoming" German, even through generations of assimilation.[6]

Despite such efforts to freeze racial definitions irrevocably, the boundaries do shift for both mainstream and extremist racial identities, but the process of change typically requires generations. Short of hiding one's ancestry in order to enter an in-group (known as *passing*), out-group members have no option to become a full member of the in-group.

The character of a racial extremist movement is influenced somewhat by whether the racial in-group is a majority or a minority in its host society, but both types exist. For instance, a variety of white and black nationalist movements can be found in the United States.

Extremism requires an unwavering commitment to hostile actions against an out-group, discussed in more detail later in this chapter. Majority in-groups may incorrectly characterize minority groups as extremist for seeking equal protection under the law or the redress of legitimate grievances. For instance, some right-wing extremists in the United States accuse the Black Lives Matter movement of extremism, but there is nothing inherently extremist about campaigning for equal protection under the law.

Religious

Most religions stipulate that their beliefs and practices are objectively superior to all others. Members of religious out-groups usually suffer some penalty for their wrong beliefs, but the penalty is often intangible, whether it is exclusion from a paradise in the afterlife, reincarnation in an inferior position, or an expectation that out-group members will fail to achieve enlightenment and peace.

In contrast, religious extremists impose penalties on out-groups here in the temporal world. As with racial extremism, these penalties can include shunning, discriminatory practices, and even extermination. The establishment of a theocratic state typically falls somewhere on the extremist spectrum because most theocracies penalize nonbelievers by forcing them to adhere to values and practices they do not share or subjecting them to discrimination or oppression.

Unlike racial extremists, religious extremists usually include some established mechanism whereby members of the out-group can join the in-group through conversion, whether voluntarily or under threat, using a relatively consistent procedure. Indeed, extremist groups often contain disproportionate numbers of converts. In this sense, religious extremism can be seen as slightly less intractable than racial extremism, although religious extremists are nevertheless capable of the same extraordinary violence and intolerance.

Nationalist

Nationalism is typically understood as promoting the interests of one's own nation over the interests of others or the world at large, typically joined with a feeling of superiority to other nations. It is normal and even healthy for an engaged citizen to experience a certain amount of nationalist sentiment—such as feeling proud or grateful to be an American.

Nationalist extremism takes this to a different level, arguing that the nation must be protected by taking hostile action against out-groups. Sometimes this means taking action against other nations or the world at large, but nationalist extremism is frequently concerned with immigration—how citizenship is defined and bestowed.

Because of this, nationalist extremism is often paired, implicitly or explicitly, with the idea of racial or religious restrictions on who can become a citizen. Over the course of its history, the United States has experienced several such waves of nationalist extremism, manifesting in hostility toward immigrants from a variety of ethnic and religious backgrounds.

Today, many American nationalist extremists are fixated primarily on Muslims, arguing that they cannot truly be Americans because their first loyalty is to Islam. A similar debate took place earlier in American history regarding Roman Catholics and their perceived allegiance to the pope.[7] Although many anti-Muslim extremists are Christian and believe they are defending America's identity as a Christian nation, there are notable exceptions, including Jews and atheists who oppose Muslim immigration for other reasons. This results in a sort of hybrid nationalism, with a somewhat amorphous national identity in-group standing in opposition to a specific religious or racial out-group.

As with religion, there are established procedures for members of the out-group to join the in-group and acquire citizenship. But although religious conversion is often accepted and even embraced by religious extremists, nationalists often aim their ire and political activism at the procedures surrounding citizenship, seeking to restrict or even eliminate them.

However, not all conversations about establishing orderly rules for citizenship and the enforcement of immigration laws are extremist in nature. Extremism becomes an issue when those conversations revolve around targeting current and prospective immigrants for hostile measures.

Anti-government

For antigovernment extremists, the out-group is the government of the country in which they live. Often but not always, antigovernment ideologies are tied to a belief that a country's founding values or principles have been corrupted. The government and those who support it are enemy out-groups. In-groups are less clearly defined. For some, the in-groups are an archetype of the ordinary citizen. For others, the in-group consists only of other people who share specific values or recognize the illegitimacy of the existing government. As with nationalist extremism, the government out-group may be tied to a racial or religious dimension. For instance, many American antigovernment extremists believe that the corruption of the United States government is the result of a Jewish conspiracy.[8]

Anarchist

Anarchists differ from antigovernment extremists in that they are opposed to all forms of compulsory government rather than only a specific existing regime. Instead, anarchists believe that people should participate in society on a voluntary and spontaneously organized basis. Simply holding this belief does not make people extremists unless they also believe that they must take hostile action against existing governments and political participants.

As one might expect, the anti-organizational nature of anarchism makes it difficult to mount large and cohesive movements, but anarchist extremism was a violent force to be reckoned with in the late nineteenth century and throughout much of the twentieth, credited with assassinating many leaders of major Western powers, including Russian tsar Alexander II, French president Marie François Sadi Carnot, U.S. president William McKinley, Spanish king Umberto I and Austrian empress Elisabeth.[9]

Classist

Most people have heard the phrase *class warfare*, and many have probably rolled their eyes at it. Conflicts over class are not typically classified as extremism, although class is often a crucial part of conflicts among other identity types.

However, class is a highly fungible commodity, volatile and significantly dependent on perception and relative status. People move in and out of classes far more easily than other identities, and a class-based movement is difficult to sustain, in part because successful movements result in a sweeping redefinition of in-groups and out-groups. Although serious class-based conflicts can overturn the class structure entirely, as in the Russian Revolution, they are often about moving groups of people from one class to another or adjusting their relative status, which does not lend itself to an unwavering need for hostile action based on clear categories, a component of the definition of extremism presented later in this chapter.

Certain ideologies, such as Communism, are explicitly class-based and may take on an extremist dimension, as in the case of Marxist or Maoist terrorism, which (in principle, at least) seek to eliminate the existence of an upper class.[10] Class-based ideologies may also be hybridized with other ideologies, as in the case of anarchist socialism and anarcho-syndicalism[11] or in racial extremist movements in societies where race and class are closely related categories.

Single-Issue Movements
A variety of movements carry out terrorist attacks or other violence on the basis of single issues. These groups may formulate an identity construct as part of their ideology but may not be fully formed as extremist movements. Generally, for these movements, the in-group is made up of people who are on the right side of the single issue, and the out-group is made up of people who are on the wrong side. In some cases, these movements may be an ambiguous fit with the definition offered later in this chapter.

For instance, some anti-abortion violence is motivated in a relatively simple way by the belief that a fetus is fully human and alive. It is not surprising that people who hold that belief would turn to violence to prevent what they see as murder. But other people who carry out violence around abortion and reproductive rights are motivated by wider ideologies related to religion or the role of women in society.

Although less common, pro- and antitechnology extremists surface from time to time. Most famously, Ted Kaczynski, better known as the Unabomber, carried out a series of parcel bombings to advance his view that technology is bad for society and human happiness. Kaczynski's case is unusual in that he represented a one-man movement, but he still identified an out-group—leftists, a word that appears in Kaczynski's manifesto 126 times as both contributor to and manifestation of technology's ill effects.

Other examples of single-issue or limited-scope movements include tax protestors and antifascists (known as antifa), although adherents of these movements may adopt additional out-group categories and incorporate elements of other ideologies. For tax protestors, this usually includes antigovernment extremism, whereas antifa adherents often embrace some form of anarchism.

Environmental and animal rights movements are among the most prolific users of terrorism in pursuit of a political goal, although their attacks have typically been far less lethal than those of other extremists. Generally speaking, in recent years left-wing extremists have produced far fewer fatalities than right-wing and jihadist extremists, although that has not always been true from a historical perspective.[12]

Gender, Sexual Orientation, and Sexual Identity

Perhaps the most intimate and powerful identities in human experience revolve around gender and sexual orientation. It is not surprising, therefore, that these identities are often a central focus for extremists. Some extremist movements center on these specific identities—such as so-called Men's Rights Activists (MRAs) who promote an agenda that is distinctly antiwoman or advocates of "conversion therapy" who use fraudulent and torturous techniques to "cure" gay people.[13]

In addition to movements that are centrally concerned with gender and sexual identity, many extremist movements rely on these issues incidentally or as part of a wider ideology. Gender and sexual identity are often featured as an add-on component to some other form of ideological extremism.

Strict enforcement of gender and sexual mores often features prominently in extremist ideologies that are chiefly concerned with some other primary identity. Although both men and women take part in extremism, men are overwhelmingly overrepresented in extremist populations, especially where the commission of acts of violence are concerned. Women do participate in extremist movements at many levels, but they are sharply underrepresented in leadership and violent action roles.[14] This has at times led scholars and policymakers to underplay women's involvement, but the overrepresentation of males (usually cisgender heterosexual males) as active participants is clear and persistent.[15]

Some extremist ideologies, particularly on the far right and in jihadist circles, relegate women to nonviolent roles and emphasize their reproductive function as a core contribution to the movement. In other words, they urge women to bear and raise children as a way to propagate the in-group. Male extremists' control over women may be explicit or implicit, but it is rarely invisible. This often results in various forms of fetishization of women, as seen in white nationalist propaganda claiming "white women are magic" and featuring stylized pictures of white mothers with many white children.[16]

Islamic State has featured women in its propaganda and employed them as recruiters on social media, encouraging women to migrate to territories under its control in order to marry the organization's fighters. Within its territory, Islamic State has established women's brigades to violently enforce extreme social mores against other women.[17] Even more disturbingly, Islamic State has openly institutionalized sexual slavery and rape against members of the Yazidi minority group in Iraq, as an incentive for male in-group members.[18]

Conversely, one of the most ubiquitous themes in extremist propaganda is the threat of rape—real or imagined—by out-group males against in-group females. This is a powerful emotional manipulation tactic for mobilizing male in-group extremists, who are most likely to commit violence. This theme is repeated endlessly by extremist propagandists, often in stark and emotionally evocative terms.[19]

Attitudes toward sexual identity in right-wing and jihadist circles are similarly conscribed. Islamic State punished homosexuality in its circles by stoning gay men or throwing them from the tops of buildings.[20] Within right-wing circles, deviations from cisgender heterosexuality are usually shunned or persecuted, with the most extreme example being Nazi campaigns that sent thousands of gay men to concentration camps, with some being castrated and others subjected to medical experiments in search of a "cure."[21]

During the 1980s, American right-wing extremists operated a dial-in computerized bulletin board to maintain a list of gay men who would be targeted during a future uprising.[22] Others defined homosexuality as a "mental illness." But by the 1990s, some ambiguity began to surface in white nationalist prescriptions for how to deal with lesbian, gay, bisexual, transgender, and questioning (LG-BTQ) individuals, with views ranging violent suppression to viewing homosexuality as a minor vice comparable to prostitution, "tolerated but not accepted."[23]

There are important exceptions, especially in recent years. During the 2010s, the rise of the extremist alt-right movement brought with it a notable trend toward conditional acceptance of some LGBTQ community members—so long as they shared the movement's signature anti-Muslim and anti-immigrant views. However, most within the movement continued to support strict antigay and antitrans policies.[24]

Extremism: A Working Definition

Extremism is incredibly diverse, even though most extremist movements attempt to suppress diversity on racial, religious, or ideological grounds. Given the range of movements that differ so much from each other, how do we approach the study of extremism as a discrete discipline? How do we do better than "we know it we see it"?

The answer lies in distinguishing between the structure and the content of extremist ideologies. The contents of different extremist ideologies are wildly inconsistent. Pro-Muslim and anti-Muslim extremists, for example, are diametrically opposed with respect to the content of their beliefs, yet they are remarkably similar with respect to the structure of what they believe and how they justify their views.

The chapters that follow describe that structure, which consists of two symbiotic notions. First, formulaic in-group and out-group definitions flesh out identities, and second, a crisis-solution construct prescribes action based on those identity definitions. The structure allows for a significant amount of variation, while also providing for relatively succinct definitions of extremism and radicalization that encompass most of the examples discussed so far.[25] For purposes of this book, the following definitions apply.

Extremism refers to the belief that an in-group's success or survival can never be separated from the need for hostile action against an out-group. The hostile action must be part of the in-group's definition of success. Hostile acts can range from verbal attacks and diminishment to discriminatory behavior, violence, and even genocide. This is obviously a very wide spectrum of activity, which will be discussed in more detail in the following chapters.

Extremism can be the province of state or nonstate actors, unlike terrorism, which after years of similar debate and ambiguity, has come to be understood primarily as a nonstate phenomenon.[26]

Each component of this definition is important, since not every harmful or violent act is necessarily extremist.

Competition according to a set of negotiated rules is not usually extremist, because in-group success (winning) can be separated from harmful, out-of-bounds acts against competitors (such as persecution, sabotage or assassination). This applies to such pursuits as politics, sports, or business. The need for harmful activity must be unconditional and inseparable from the in-group's understanding of success in order to qualify as extremist.

For instance, most white nationalists believe that white people can never be successful unless and until nonwhites are removed from in-group society by means of segregation or extermination. This demand is definitional, non-negotiable and unconditional. To abandon the demand would be to abandon white nationalism.

In contrast, conditional conflicts are not necessarily extremist. For instance, if a nation is attacked through an act of war, hostile action may become a legitimate necessity in order to ensure the survival of the in-group, but that necessity can be conditional. The in-group becomes extremist if it insists that hostile action must continue unconditionally, for instance by insisting on the extermination of out-group members after they have surrendered.

The call to action is inherent to this definition. For instance, it is not extremist to disapprove of a religion based on its tenets. But it is extremist to demand that all adherents of a religion be arrested or deported.

Finally, the definition is dependent on an assertion of identity. Societies are entitled to craft laws regulating behavior, for instance by establishing a minimum age for marriage, and these rules may conflict with the rules of some group identities. It is not extremist to differ over values. But laws crafted specifically to target an out-group identity—for instance, Jim Crow laws enforcing segregation, or laws restricting religious belief—are extremist under this definition. The question of intent leads to some unavoidable gray areas, but evaluating legal and political decisions against the other components of this definition can help clarify the question in many cases.

Violent extremism is the belief that an in-group's success or survival can never be separated from the need for violent action against an out-group (as opposed to less harmful acts such as discrimination or shunning). A violent extremist ideology may characterize its violence as defensive, offensive, or preemptive. Here again, inseparability is the key element—a stipulation that the need for violence against an out-group is not conditional or situational. War is not automatically extremist, but a genocidal war is.

Radicalization into extremism is the escalation of an in-group's extremist orientation in the form of increasingly negative views about an out-group or the endorsement of increasingly hostile or violent actions against an out-group. Radicalization is a process of change, not outcome.

The lack of scholarly consensus about what *extremism* and *radicalization* mean virtually guarantees that these definitions will prove controversial in some quarters. These definitions are less subjective than most that preceded them, but it is impossible to eliminate all gray areas. In my view, these definitions combine the flexibility to cross ideological lines with enough specificity to counter the often subjective use of the terms.

Extremism as a Spectrum

As the definition of *radicalization into extremism* suggests, extremism represents a spectrum of beliefs rather than a fixed destination. With good reason, policymakers and activists most often focus on violent extremism. Violence is the most destructive, escalatory, and irrevocable expression of the extremist paradigm. But not all extremist movements begin and end with violence.

Extremism emerges from social ecosystems in a manner analogous to weather. No two hurricanes are exactly alike, but we can recognize them when they form, follow them through stages, and estimate their future behavior—imperfectly. But we cannot understand hurricanes if we do not understand tropical storms, and we cannot understand storms if we do not understand wind and water. In the same way, we need to understand the component elements that make up extremist ideologies in order to understand how extremist movements work.

Few movements are born extreme. Most emerge from mainstream identities that affirm the merits of an in-group—pride in a heritage or the values of a religion—without stipulating that the in-group must take hostile action against an out-group. Out-group definitions evolve over time, starting with categorization (exclusion from the in-group) and escalating as the in-group develops a more and more negative view of the out-group.

Chapter 3 examines how identity movements define and subdivide in-groups and out-groups. Chapter 4 examines how these elements are forged into a crisis-solution narrative that drives violence and other hostile interactions among collectives.

Additional Reading

As part of the MIT Press's Essential Knowledge series, which is intended to offer concise, accessible overviews of compelling topics, this book is relatively brief and focuses on broad concepts. Some readers, particularly academics and those working in the fields of counterterrorism and countering violent extremism, may be interested in exploring more thorough explanations of this framework for extremism and how it was developed.

While this text includes case studies to illustrate various aspects of the framework, they are necessarily brief. Therefore, a detailed bibliography is included at the end of the book with guidance for finding more comprehensive explanations and grounded theory explorations tied to sections of the book. The bibliography includes significant books and papers that explain the origins of concepts discussed here and provide detailed evidence from primary sources (extremist ideological and propaganda texts). I will continue to publish new research and analysis regarding this framework, and an up-to-date list of my work, with links, can always be found at www.jmberger.com.

IN-GROUPS AND OUT-GROUPS

The act of joining a movement is an assertion of identity, and thus, membership in a movement always begins with a statement of "We believe" or simply "We are." The most basic element of collective identity is the in-group, the people who "belong." In-groups often form organically based on obvious connections. For instance, people who are born and live in Boston may consider themselves Bostonians. Not everyone who lives in a place will identify with the local collective, but it's an easy, obvious, and typically useful identity.

There is nothing inherently objectionable about joining an in-group, and such identification is often a positive act. Strong identification with a national in-group may be lauded as patriotism. Strong identification with a religious in-group may be described as devotion. Strong identification with an ethnic in-group may be described as pride in one's heritage.

But research also shows that joining an in-group can set the stage for less admirable behavior. Many studies suggest that the mere act of identifying with an in-group makes people more susceptible to biases that favor their peers and denigrate members of out-groups.[1]

After the criteria for membership in the in-group have been identified, the existence of out-groups naturally follows. Someone who has never lived in Boston is excluded from the Bostonian in-group. People from New York, for instance, are part of an out-group for Bostonians.

But for many Bostonians, the basic geographic test for in-group membership is only the tip of the iceberg. Some Bostonians will gladly list the many ways in which Bostonians and New Yorkers diverge—including accents, style of dress, and the qualities of their sports teams. These differences are sometimes highlighted as reasons for mockery or dislike, and animus runs in both directions, although it is usually lighthearted.

The boundaries between in-group and out-group identities are often vague, highly subjective, and changeable over time. For instance, if you live in Boston for forty years and then live in New York for ten years, you may still consider yourself a Bostonian. If you live in New York for twenty-five years and then live in Boston for fifteen, you may consider yourself a Bostonian, but some Bostonians will consider you a New Yorker.

Over time and in particular contexts, the definition of *Bostonian* may expand to refer to people living in the greater Boston area, including suburbs. But when people within that in-group talk to each other, specific neighborhood identities may emerge as preferable to the broader metropolitan identity. How individuals categorize themselves is often context-dependent. You might identify as a Bostonian when speaking to a New Yorker, for example, but as a resident of South Boston when speaking to someone from another neighborhood, like the North End.

This subjectivity and changeability can make it very difficult to determine who's in your in-group and who's out. Extremist movements are overwhelmingly concerned with taking the subjectivity out of that question. They seek to eliminate gray areas and clearly define the following:

- What makes an individual part of the in-group

- Why the in-group has legitimacy

- What makes an individual part of the out-group

- Why the out-group is less legitimate than the in-group

• How members of the in-group should interact with members of the out-group.

The last element is perhaps the most important distinction between mainstream and extremist identities. When the stakes of in-group and out-group membership are low, the question of legitimacy is trivial, and peaceful coexistence rules the day. Bostonians who move to New York might be teased at family gatherings—maybe even taunted at sporting events. But these identities are not typically a matter of life and death.

Defining the In-Group

Identity starts at home. It is almost impossible to live in society without passively absorbing or actively adopting membership in some sort of in-group. You may not think of yourself primarily in terms of being white, for instance, but that affiliation will impact how other members of society interact with you during a job interview or a traffic stop.

When an identity grouping evolves beyond matters of convenience and simplicity, such as demarcating where you live or go to school, it requires a narrative to explain the meaning of the collective—what the identity means, where it comes from, and where it is going. An in-group definition describes a prototypical or archetypical in-group member, defined by three major elements:[2]

- **Beliefs:** The shared creed of an in-group, most importantly its values, but including secondary elements such as cosmology or metaphysics.

- **Traits:** Descriptive qualities that apply to in-group members, including physical (such as skin tone or hair type), mental (intelligence or creativity), social (dialect, slang, and accents), or spiritual (virtuousness or piety).

- **Practices:** What members of the in-group do and how they are expected to behave, including:

  - *Past behavior:* The group's history

  - *Current behavior:* How the group conducts itself today

  - *Future behavior:* The group's destiny

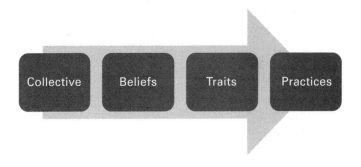

Figure 1   Elements of group definition

Defining these qualities takes time, and not all identity groups will fill out every part of this narrative. But most of them eventually emerge in some form. Being born in Boston may be enough to qualify you as Bostonian, but committed Bostonians know how things are done their city. They know and cherish the history of Boston's role in the Revolutionary War, they know what kind of chowder should be served, and they speak using wicked local slang.

As details accumulate, an identity becomes more distinct from others. When this collection of details begins to congeal into a historical and contemporary narrative— when it stops being a list of facts and starts being the "story of us"—it becomes a powerful tool for establishing legitimacy and group cohesion.[3]

After this identity narrative is established, it becomes self-reinforcing. History (whether true or mythologized) is initially used to construct an identity. But then identity becomes the filter through which subsequent, motivated histories are written, a cycle that synchronizes history and identity as a unified understanding.[4]

Defining the Out-Group

The mere existence of an out-group does not automatically signal that an in-group has moved to extremism. An identity movement does not become extreme until the in-group starts to adopt hostile attitudes toward the out-group or -groups. For this to happen, the out-groups must also be clearly defined through a narrative process of identity construction that parallels the construction of the in-group definition—a template that includes a description of the out-group's beliefs, traits, and practices (past, present, and future). In contrast to in-groups, out-groups tend to be defined in negative tones.

Importantly, the sources of information used to define the out-group tend to be less reliable. Members of an in-group directly experience their personal beliefs and their current practices (although those experiences may be selective and incomplete). In contrast, information about out-group beliefs and practices usually includes a mix of truth, interpretation, and fiction. As a movement shifts toward extremism, this mix may shift toward fiction and become more toxic, aggressively highlighting negative data points and ignoring or rebutting positive data points.

Case Study: British Israelism

The origins of the white nationalist movement known as Christian Identity illustrate how in-group identity narratives are filled out. Christian Identity is a racist outgrowth of a nineteenth-century movement known as British

Israelism, which argued that Anglo-Saxons were the descendants of the Lost Tribes of Israel.

Jewish and Christian scriptures describe the nation of Israel as including twelve tribes, but only two are accounted for in history after about the eighth century BCE. Over time, the fate of the remaining ten tribes inspired intense religious speculation and mythmaking. A dizzying array of speculative historical theories have identified many different ethnic groups as alleged descendants of the Lost Tribes, including Anglo-Saxons, Native Americans, Pakistanis, Indians, the Maori, the Japanese, and Africans from several different regions and nations, as well as everyone under the heading "black."[5]

For the British Israelists, the claimed ethnic link between the Lost Tribes and Anglo-Saxony was originally intended to identify the British Empire as heir to biblical prophecies about a divinely blessed "company of nations." Under British Israelist theory, the United States was associated with the tribe of Manasseh, prophesied to become a "great nation" in parallel to the Empire.[6] British Israelists asserted a historical theory that the British Empire and the United States were—genetically and factually, not metaphorically—the nation of Israel in modern times and thus heir to God's promises.

The ideology began as an effort to enhance the legitimacy of the in-group, Anglo-Saxony, by tracing its genealogy to the Lost Tribes. British Israel theorists framed this as an explicitly racial theory that accorded preferential status to Anglo-Saxons, but their initial narratives also united Anglo-Saxons and ethnic Jews in a shared Semitic heritage.[7]

The argument for British Israelism was neither simple nor obvious, so its adherents had to construct narrative justifications to define the in-group and establish its legitimacy. In other words, they had to tell a convincing story about how this convergence between Anglo-Saxony and the sacred state of Israel came to be, and they did so by writing hundreds of lengthy tomes on the topic.

British Israelist writers began by citing scriptures that focus on the extensive genealogies found in the Old Testament. They argued that the events and family trees described in the Bible show that the kingship of Israel and the benefit of God's covenants had passed to members of the Lost Tribes rather than to modern-day Jews. Elaborating from this starting point, they then employed a mix of history, folklore, and legend to link Anglo-Saxons with the Lost Tribes.[8]

The early authors acknowledged and even embraced a kinship between Anglo-Saxons and Jews, but British Israelism contained implicit tensions with Judaism. The prevalent Christian view of the day was that the coming of Jesus had invalidated God's covenants with Israel and the Jews. From the perspective of the authors, British Israelism restored the validity of those covenants, renewed the status of God's "chosen people," and extended the covenants to include Anglo-Saxons. From a British Israelist perspective, this didn't take anything away from Jewish people that had not already been lost.

From a Jewish perspective, however, these pacts with God had never been invalidated, so the move to add Anglo-Saxons as the beneficiary of Jewish covenants smacked of disenfranchisement, especially because British Israelist authors unanimously agreed that the Jews would have to convert to Christianity in order to participate fully in the fulfillment of prophecies and the hegemony of the company of nations.[9]

British Israelist theory began as a seemingly innocuous exercise to enhance in-group legitimacy. But it also contained the seeds of a Jewish out-group. If the British Empire was the rightful state of Israel, then the conclusion followed that anyone else claiming that mantle must be illegitimate. The creation of a Jewish state of Israel in the 1940s therefore precipitated a crisis for the movement, eventually leading to the creation of a successor ideology—the violently anti-Semitic movement known as Christian Identity.

The example of British Israelism also drives home an important point about extremist identities: they are fluid. Although extremists laboriously work to crystallize the definition of the in-group in any given moment, over time the definitions change in response to shifting circumstances. For instance, as British Israelism became

Christian Identity, the in-group definition shifted from Anglo-Saxon to a more broadly defined "white" race that included other ethnicities, such as Scandinavians and Teutonic Germans.

Dividing the In-Group

For most people, personal identity consists of overlapping circles of belonging, such as "I am an American, and I am also ethnically Irish, and I am also Roman Catholic, and I am also an environmental activist." The components of any given person's sense of identity may be complementary, neutral, or contradictory: "I am a Democrat, but I am also a gun-rights advocate"; "I am a Republican, but I am also pro-choice."

For extremists, a singular identity often emerges from these circles of belonging. Some identities are conflated into a unified construct ("I am an American, but America is a Christian nation"), and others become fully exclusive ("I am not an Iraqi because I am a Muslim first").

Extremist ideologies define constrictive or exclusive identities and enforce rigid boundaries between in-groups and out-groups. Ironically, this quest to promote greater group cohesion can itself fracture the in-group. Shared negative attitudes toward outsiders can help strengthen bonds around certain in-group members,[10] but they also put pressure on members of the in-group to adopt more hostile attitudes toward the out-group. When this happens, the unity of the in-group comes under pressure.

Remember that most broad identities are not extremist. It's not extremist to identify as Anglo-Saxon or African American, Christian, or Muslim. Extremist movements like Christian Identity and Islamic State sprout from these broad identities, but they quickly take on their own distinct character.

When an extremist identity emerges, it must recruit adherents from the broader identity group from which it came. This process requires extremists to divide the in-group into subcategories. As extremist movements form robust organizational structures and begin to recruit, these subcategories take on surpassing importance.

A mature extremist organization must address three crucial subdivisions in its ideological formulations:

• **Extremist in-group:** The extremist movement or organization itself. For a highly developed movement like Islamic State, this category may include both formal members and active supporters.

• **Eligible in-group:** The broad identity collective that an extremist organization claims to represent and from which it seeks to recruit. For Islamic State, the eligible in-group consists of Sunni Muslims. All Sunni Muslims are eligible to join the Islamic State. The extremist group often believes it represents the purest iteration of the eligible group.

• **Ineligible in-group:** In-group members who are at risk of being expelled from the in-group, in the view of an extremist movement. When members of the eligible in-group reject the extremist movement, extremists may in turn seek to eject them from the eligible in-group. As an extremist movement becomes more developed, it begins to treat eligibility as obligation. In other words, a group like Islamic State believes not only that Sunni Muslims are *eligible* to join its movement but that they are *obligated* to do so.[11] For example, Islamic State often declares Sunni Muslims who oppose its teachings and tactics to be apostate from the religion of Islam as a whole.

For movements that have not yet become extreme or that have not yet formed a discrete organization, subdivisions of the in-group may be underdefined or entirely undefined. The distinction between ineligible in-group and out-group can be blurry. In some instances, ineligible in-group members may be classified as the extremist organization's functional out-group—serving as the primary or sole focus of the extremist in-group's ire. Attitudes toward the ineligible in-group can be more hostile and violent than toward a more distinct out-group, due to the ineligible's "betrayal," which cannot be explained by ignorance. Typically, the ineligible group carries both the stigma of treason and the possibility of redemption.

In contrast, the extremist in-group has stark boundaries with little tolerance for passivity. The extremist in-group is almost universally framed by belief in its own **purity,** which in this context means the measure of how closely an in-group conforms to the prototypical in-group identity described by an ideology. Members of the extremist in-group see themselves as the epitome of the eligible in-group—its purest expression, unpolluted by the ideological or racial influence of out-groups. Adherents often stipulate that members of the eligible in-group must purify themselves before joining the extremist in-group, bringing their individual identities in line with the prototype.

As an extremist movement accrues meaningful numbers of followers and begins recruiting, these categories become critically important. In order to attract members, an extremist organization must make an urgent, two-part argument that demonizes the out-group and requires eligible people to become extremists (discussed in chapter 4).

Case Study: Heresiology

During the youngest days of Christianity, there was no singular definition of what it meant to be a follower of Jesus

Christ and therefore part of the Christian in-group. In the religion's first few centuries, a variety of competing views and sects emerged, ranging from a traditionalist Jewish interpretation of Jesus as a nondivine prophet through the complex and esoteric cosmologies of Gnosticism.[12]

At some point, these beliefs began to emerge as an identity called "Christian," which quickly became exclusive of other identities, such as Jewish or pagan. As Christian beliefs spread geographically, they evolved in different and often conflicting directions. Christian leaders soon became eager to winnow these competing creeds into one "true" religion.

As part of that process, they crystallized a relatively recent concept known as **heresy** or **apostasy**, the belief that substantially wrong beliefs or practices can disqualify an otherwise eligible person from an in-group. In mainstream theology, heresy and apostasy are different concepts, with the former referring to wrong religious belief within an in-group, and the latter referring to a complete repudiation of the in-group.[13] In extremism, these terms are often conflated, because extremists believe that certain kinds of wrong belief are equivalent to an explicit repudiation of the in-group.

Early Christian heresy-hunters included Justin Martyr, whose writings on the subject have been lost to time, and Irenaeus, whose writings have survived in part. Justin and Irenaeus lumped together various Christian sects as "evil" in-group factions that were influenced by Satan to oppose an emerging in-group orthodoxy, a proto-version of Roman Catholic canon that claimed to represent the only correct version of Christian belief.[14]

Irenaeus authored a five-volume treatise, *Against Heresies*, intended to strengthen in-group cohesion by clearly defining which practices and beliefs were orthodox (part of the correct in-group definition) and which were not. Those who deviated from his proposed orthodoxy and refused to accept correction were ineligible in-group members—"heretics" or "apostates" infected by Satan's influence.

Ineligible in-group members must be opposed, Irenaeus wrote, through strong and persistent refutation, a mild prescription.[15] But his framing of heresy and apostasy set the stage for more assertive definitions of identity to come. After the emperor Constantine orchestrated the codification the orthodoxy of the Christian Church under the Roman Empire, his successors took steps to make that orthodoxy legally binding in the Edict of Thessalonica, also known as *Cunctos populos* (All the people). Issued in 380 CE, the edict established Catholicism as the official state religion of the Roman Empire.

To be fully recognized by the state, citizens were required to acknowledge the truth of orthodox doctrine. Those who refused were "to be punished not only by divine retribution, but also by our own measures," meaning penalties under the law. Later edicts explicitly put the secular might of the Roman Empire at the service of the pope for the enforcement of orthodox norms.[16]

Soon after the issuance of the *Cunctos populos*, John Chrysostom, a fourth-century archbishop of Constantinople, delivered a series of speeches titled "Against the Jews" that criticized Christian sectarians who still observed Jewish practices and associated with Jewish communities. While his primary target was the ineligible in-group, he based much of his refutation on a condemnation of the Jewish out-group. Chrysostom detailed many lurid charges against Jews, including accusations that they sacrificed children to demons.[17]

"If you admire the Jewish way of life, what do you have in common with us?" he admonished his fellow Christians.[18] Chrysostom urged his followers to emulate him in "hating" and shunning the Jews and those Christians who maintained Judaic practices such as fasting. He urged adherents to confront and rebuke other Christians who mixed with Jews—even beating them if they did not accept verbal correction. If violence failed to enforce in-group norms, those who refused to see the light should be expelled from the Christian community.[19] Ironically, Chrysostom himself died in exile under the specter of heresy, although his reputation was later rehabilitated.[20]

Extremism is a spectrum of beliefs, not necessarily a simple destination.

Should these church fathers, who are now remembered as saints, be understood as extremists? Extremism is a spectrum of beliefs, not necessarily a simple destination. Few historians would cite Irenaeus as an example of extremism as we understand it today, but his role in elevating the concept of heresy had dramatic ramifications for the trajectory of the church, both in the short term and over the long term, and for later concepts of heresy in Judaism, Islam, and other religions.

In-group conflicts are an inevitable part of establishing orthodoxy, and Irenaeus was clearly concerned with that process. Chrysostom's writings are more problematic. While his stated goal was to correct the practices of ineligible in-group members, his sermons employed calls to violence and a full-throated attack on Jews as an enemy out-group. With good reason, Chrysostom is understood by many to be an important figure in the history of anti-Semitism, although that understanding is neither simple nor universal.

Whether or not these men fit our preconceptions about extremists, their early exercises in group definition helped set the stage for bloodier Christian assaults on heretics and other out-groups in the centuries to come, first in the form of raids and mob violence by Christians against pagans and Jews and later, more insidiously, in the form of the Crusades and the Inquisition.[21]

The Epistemology of Identity

Identities are often formed out of convenience and circumstance, but they don't exist in a meaningful way until they are asserted. Identities are created, not found, and so the process by which they are assembled is important. Each group definition—in and out—is a template waiting to be filled with information about beliefs, traits, and practices. The sources for this information shape the attitudes of the group.

We obtain information in two ways—through direct experience (what happens to us) and by transmission (what others tell us). Experience and transmission are both subjective, but transmission is especially susceptible to honest misunderstanding, accidental misinformation, and intentional manipulation.

Members of an in-group usually experience in-group beliefs, traits, and current practices directly. They receive information about past practices via transmission—for instance, in the form of scriptures or written histories. Practices are usually the most salient element for extremist ideologues to emphasize because in-group practices most clearly define identity and out-group practices most clearly define a threat to the in-group (see chapter 4).

In-group members rely even more heavily on transmitted information about out-groups. The nature of categorization imposes a distance between the in-group and out-group, heightening the role of narratives in understanding the out-group. Narratives become even more important for in-groups evolving toward extremism, as in-group members are urged or commanded to shun contact with the out-group, depriving themselves of data points that might contradict their increasingly negative views.

This effect is highly dependent on context.[22] Overall, research strongly suggests that direct interactions between social groups tend to undercut negative views.[23] For example, polling of American views on Muslims found that people who personally knew Muslims were less inclined to have negative views about them.[24]

But in-group members who have powerfully negative personal experiences with out-group members (such as racial discrimination or a violent encounter) can adopt very negative views about the out-group as a whole. Someone who has a traumatic personal experience with an out-group may search for explanations, making them more susceptible to transmitted narratives that contextualize what happened.[25]

Taboos that inhibit or prohibit direct contact between in-groups and out-groups create a rhetorical space in which constructed narratives about the out-group can proliferate and gain power. These narratives rely on transmitted information, including the following:

Taboos that inhibit or prohibit direct contact between in-groups and out-groups create a rhetorical space in which constructed narratives about the out-group can proliferate and gain power.

- Information about the past, such as

  - Real or consensus history

  - Interpreted or revisionist history

  - Unverified histories, such as scriptures, myth and folklore, and fictionalized histories or historical fiction

- Information about the present, such as

  - Real news

  - Fake news or fiction

  - Conspiracy theories

  - Analysis

  - Opinion

- Projections about the future, such as

  - Analysis

  - Prophecy

  - Dystopian or apocalyptic fiction

These information sources shape the definition of each group. As an identity movement escalates toward extremism, the gap between the perceived merit of the in-group and the perfidy of the out-group grows into a chasm.

CRISES AND SOLUTIONS

It's normal for social collectives to divide themselves into in-groups and out-groups, and it's sadly common for in-groups to develop negative attitudes toward out-groups. It's normal for in-groups and out-groups to experience conflict, whether that means competing for resources, clashing over values, or even fighting the occasional war. These commonplace events are not usually extremist in nature. Most conflicts are situational and transitory, even when they involve bigotry and hate.

Extremism is distinguished from ordinary unpleasantness—blind hate and pedestrian racism—by its sweeping rationalization of why conflict exists and its insistence on the necessity of conflict. It goes beyond dislike or prejudice. Extremism is related to prejudice, but it is a distinct problem. It is an assertion that an out-group must always be actively opposed because its fundamental identity is intrinsically harmful to the in-group.

The nature of that opposition falls on a spectrum ranging from less damaging measures (such as verbal abuse or shunning) to extraordinary tactics (such as internment and genocide). Tactical and temporary truces are possible, but extremists believe the in-group's success is inseparable from hostile action toward the out-group. Permanent peace cannot be achieved until the out-group has been decisively dominated or destroyed, an outcome that is rarely achievable. In the rare event that an out-group is effectively destroyed, an extremist in-group will almost always seek to initiate conflict with new out-groups. For instance, after the extermination of the Cathars in the Albigensian Crusade (chapter 1), the Roman Catholic Church initiated an escalating series of Inquisitions designed to root out additional forms of heresy.

The necessity of hostile action is tied to the belief that an out-group must be impeding the in-group's success in some way, and that this impedance proceeds from the intrinsic identity of the out-group. As extremist identities are constructed, the in-group begins to see the out-group as an unmitigated threat to its legitimacy. This threat creates a **crisis**, a pivotal event that requires an active response from the in-group. The extremist in-group offers a **solution**, consisting of hostile actions against an out-group in an effort to resolve the crisis. This is the extremist value proposition.[1]

The extremist in-group offers a solution, consisting of hostile actions against an out-group in an effort to resolve the crisis. This is the extremist value proposition.

Case Study: The Extremist Template

Al Qaeda's most infamous propaganda film from the pre-September 11, 2001, era, *The State of the Ummah*, was released on videotape in early 2001. *Ummah* is an Arabic word for the global community of Muslims. A lavish extremist propaganda production by the standards of the day, the documentary is divided into three parts introduced by title cards in big, bold yellow letters.

The first part, "The State of the Muslim Ummah," starkly describes a series of interrelated crises afflicting Muslims around the world, including both real and distorted atrocities against Muslims in Afghanistan, Bosnia, Chechnya, Georgia, Kashmir, Kurdistan, Palestine, the Philippines, Somalia, Tajikstan, and other countries. It describes hundreds of thousands of Muslims being slaughtered and tens of thousands of Muslim women being raped. Muslims are depicted here as al Qaeda's eligible ingroup, and their status is painted in dire and lurid tones.

The second part, "Causes," defines al Qaeda's outgroups, including a "near" enemy (consisting of corrupt Arab regimes in Saudi Arabia and Egypt) and a "far" enemy (including Jews, Russians, and the United States, whose support props up the near enemy). This section includes extensive clips of Egyptian and Saudi wrongdoings, depicted as being carried out in collaboration with the far enemies.

The third part of the documentary is titled "The Solution" and is introduced with a clip of Osama bin Laden speaking:

> Thus if we know the disease, this is the remedy. The cure is in the Book of Allah. Hijrah [emigration] and Jihad [fighting]. ... So it is incumbent on the Muslims, especially those in leadership positions from among the faithful scholars, honest businessmen and heads of the tribes to migrate for the cause of Allah, and find a place where they can raise the banner of Jihad, and revitalize the Ummah to safeguard their religion and life. Otherwise they will lose everything.

"The solution" is not simply jihad, which in this context means violent action, but the al Qaeda organization, whose fighters are depicted training extensively in terrorist and insurgent tactics. In order for members of the Muslim in-group to access the solution, they must first join or support al Qaeda.

Crises

Ordinary problems lead to ordinary solutions. Extraordinary solutions are considered when facing a crisis perceived to be so massive that society may rise or fall depending on how it is resolved. As movements radicalize and advance on the spectrum of extremism, their negative attitudes toward out-groups grow more intense until the perceived conflict between in-group and out-group becomes so urgent that hostile action becomes mandatory. If the radicalization process continues unchecked, the nature of the proposed action becomes increasingly serious and eventually leads to violence.

As discussed in the previous chapter, once the existence of an out-group has been stipulated, it must be defined. To build the narrative of a crisis, real conflicts—such as political disputes or violent clashes between the in-group and out-group—are mixed with imagined or fabricated information. The proportion of truth to fiction varies for each extremist movement, but the mix is always present.

Extremist movements rely on several types of crisis narrative, which can be employed individually or combined. Extremist movements that survive for a significant amount of time can be expected to draw on multiple crisis narratives, concurrently or consecutively.

Normal political crises frequently appear within extremist narratives but are not typically sufficient to drive the development of an extremist ideology, because one of the primary functions of normal politics is to resolve conflicts expeditiously through bargaining and compromise.

Normal politics provides mechanisms to resolve conflicts expeditiously, but extremist movements do not seek to resolve conflicts through ordinary means.

Extremist movements do not seek to resolve conflicts through ordinary means, and they typically reject compromise. Extremist crises are predicated on the intrinsic identity of an out-group, so they cannot be solved without dominating or eliminating the out-group on a permanent basis.

Because of this deep connection between crisis and out-group identity, extremists cannot separate the need for hostile action from the success or survival of the in-group. Extremist crises are not relative or situational; they proceed implacably from the gap between in-group and out-group definitions.

The most common crisis narratives used by extremists include:

• **Impurity:** Corruption of in-group beliefs, practices or traits, sometimes including the infiltration of out-group beliefs, practices and traits

• **Conspiracy:** The belief that out-groups are engaged in secret actions to control in-group outcomes

• **Dystopia:** The belief that out-groups have successfully oriented society to disadvantage the in-group

• **Existential threat:** The belief that out-groups threaten the continued survival of the in-group

• **Apocalypse:** The belief that out-groups will precipitate a comprehensive end to history in the not-too distant future.

In addition to these crises, most of which presume the in-group faces a current disadvantage, successful extremist groups may face a crisis of **triumphalism** (the belief that the in-group successes can only be maintained by escalating hostile acts targeting out-groups).

Impurity

In the context of extremism, **purity** is the measure of how well the current in-group conforms to the prototypical in-group identity described in an ideology, including beliefs, traits and practices. Assaults on purity are often interpreted as part of a broader crisis, as described in the narratives that follow. But in some cases, purity and impurity are at the root of a crisis.

Impurity becomes a crisis when the in-group deviates from the prototypical identity, reaching critical urgency if the in-group begins to resemble the out-group in its beliefs, traits and practices. The in-group can be corrupted by excessive friendly contact or intermarriage with the out-group, or the propagation of out-group identity elements within the in-group.

For racial extremists who strictly define the in-group by heredity, impurity is an existential threat absent all other complications. Mixed relationships between races produce offspring who are disqualified from the in-group definition, and these unions are perceived as taking place at the expense of same-race couplings. Thus, modern-day white nationalists refer to race mixing as "white genocide" because they argue it reduces the available population of "pure" white people.

For religious and ideological in-groups, purity may be more complicated because the corruption believed to result from contact with the out-group is mental or spiritual in nature. For these groups, impurity is typically a component of a larger crisis.

For example, in Islamist and jihadist extremist movements, the corruption of the "pure" religion of Islam[2] is directly responsible for the suffering of Muslims, first by placing them in league with out-groups that seek to destroy them and second by encouraging *bid'ah* (religious innovation), which corrupts the purity of the in-group identity by "altering" the religion.[3]

Conspiracy

Occam's razor is a principle of analysis that states "entities are not to be multiplied beyond necessity," essentially meaning that theories should be parsimonious, stipulating only as much as is necessary to explain an observation about the world. It is commonly paraphrased as "simpler explanations are more likely to be correct."[4]

In contrast, extremists are Occam's bricklayers. They gleefully multiply entities, gravitating over time toward ever-more complex theories to explain the world in general and the nature of out-groups in particular. Conspiracy theories argue that out-groups directly control, through secretive means, the success or survival of the in-group.

Conspiracy theories are among the most powerful and ubiquitous tools that extremist ideologues use to explain real or perceived problems afflicting the in-group, attributing them to secret machinations by a powerful cabal of elite out-group members. They transfer power from an in-group to an out-group using a dyad that relentlessly drives narratives toward extremism:

- The in-group is full of merit but lacking in agency.

- The out-group lacks merit but possesses extraordinary agency.

The wide gap between these two poles creates the perception of an acute crisis that cannot be solved except through extraordinary measures. The solution to this crisis requires the creation of a parallel subset of the in-group with the power to resist the out-group—the extremist in-group, which possesses high levels of both merit and agency. The gap between merit and agency is frequently found in extremist worldviews, and a conspiracy theory is perhaps the most effective way to depict it.[5]

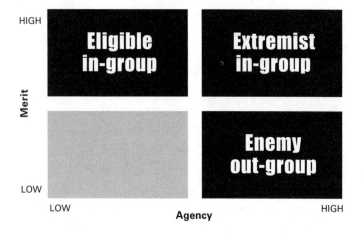

Figure 2 The distribution of merit and agency in an extremist conspiracy theory

Research suggests that conspiracy theories usually arise from the desire to provide coherent explanations for complicated problems.[6] The real world is messy, and while conspiracy theories are often arcane, they tend to be tidy. In the words of American historian Richard Hofstadter's classic 1964 essay "The Paranoid Style in American Politics,"[7] a conspiracy theory

> is nothing if not coherent—in face, the paranoid
> mentality is far more coherent than the real world,
> since it leaves no room for mistakes, failures or
> ambiguities. It is, if not wholly rational, at least

intensely rationalistic; it believes that it is up against an enemy who is as infallibly rational as he is totally evil, and it seeks to match his imputed total confidence with its own, leaving nothing unexplained and comprehending all of reality in one overreaching, consistent theory.[8]

Conspiracy theories are also cumulative, in the sense that someone who subscribes to one is likely to subscribe to more than one.[9] After a conspiracy theory enters a movement's ecosystem, more theories or more elaborations of existing theories are sure to follow. For these reasons, among others, conspiracy theories are among the most ubiquitous crisis narratives in extremist literature.

Conspiracy theories are transmitted information, as discussed in the previous chapter, but they often arise out of a desire to explain personal experiences. For instance, studies have shown that when racial in-group members directly experience a pattern of discrimination, they may be more likely to believe in conspiracy theories that explain those experiences.[10] When members of an in-group experience a disruption of the status quo, they may turn to conspiracy theories in an effort to make sense of uncertainty.

But the substance of a conspiracy theory is always transmitted, because it seeks to attribute overt events to an unseen hand that must be exposed and described. As a result, conspiracy narratives are highly susceptible to manipulation.

This effect is magnified by the fact that conspiracy theories contain an inherent element of argumentation. They are not just stories but seek to convince an audience to reach a particular conclusion.[11] Extremist ideologues put conspiracy theories at the heart of a constructed out-group identity, embellishing the description of the out-group with proliferating detail. As Hofstadter astutely observes,

> One of the impressive things about paranoid literature is precisely the elaborate concern with demonstration it almost invariably shows. ... The very fantastic character of its conclusions leads to heroic strivings for "evidence" to prove that the unbelievable is the only thing that can be believed. ... [P]aranoid literature not only starts from certain moral commitments that can be justified to many non-paranoids but also carefully and all but obsessively accumulates "evidence."[12]

Any identity group's description naturally accrues detail as time passes, but a sudden proliferation of detail may correlate to a growing extremist current.

Radicalization is ultimately concerned with expanding the divide between in-group and out-groups. So while conspiracy theories are primarily concerned with explaining out-group behavior, they represent only half of the dyad. The maximum divide occurs when the in-group is characterized as meritorious but vulnerable. As the detail of each description increases, the divide between in-group and out-group grows, sometimes with remarkable speed.

Dystopia

Dystopia is a society that has been poisoned to its core. It is corrupt, misguided, ineffectual, immoral, tyrannical, uncontrollable, or all of the above. Few crises are more profound or disturbing, which makes dystopian narratives extremely valuable for extremist ideologues and propagandists.

Many extremist narratives are broadly dystopian, an especially useful theme for terrorist and revolutionary movements that seek to overturn society at its roots. The complete destruction of the existing social order is most easily justified when the system is wholly irreparable.

Fear of dystopia can be conveyed through selective reporting of true facts. Dystopian narratives can be welded to conspiracy theories or described in fiction. Although dystopian themes feature in a wide range of extremist movements, they have been particularly effective in right-wing and racist fiction over the last two centuries, including such books as *Anticipations of the Future*, a proslavery novel published in the United States prior to the Civil War, and *The Camp of the Saints*, a racist anti-immigrant novel published in France during the 1970s. Many lesser-known examples of the dystopian fiction genre are fevered racist nightmares,[13] such as *The Turner Diaries*, a 1978 white nationalist novel in which minorities take over the United States and disarm white people. The book played a key role inspiring the Oklahoma City bombing, which killed 168 people, and dozens of other murders from the year it was written until the present.

However, dystopian narratives are by no means exclusive to right-wing movements. Jack London's 1908 socialist dystopian novel, *The Iron Heel*, advocates a violent revolution in the United States. The online hacker collective Anonymous adopted its iconic Guy Fawkes mask iconography from a 1982 to 1989 dystopian comic book series called *V for Vendetta*, which later was adapted as a movie.[14]

Dystopian stories, particularly in the form of fiction, are immersive and effective at capturing the imagination of readers. The dystopian genre has long been popular with mainstream audiences, making it attractive as an extremist recruitment and propaganda tool.[15]

In extremist dystopian narratives, the corrupt regime favors out-groups and disadvantages in-groups, often reflecting or fictionalizing conspiracy theories in a vivid format.[16] They are also a vehicle for an extremist in-group to critique the eligible in-group. Dystopian narratives often blame in-group members for weakness and acquiescence.

For example, *The Turner Diaries* devotes many pages to a critique of white Americans, blaming their passivity and lack of conviction for the emergence of the dystopian future described in the book.

Conversely, dystopian narratives, especially fictional stories set in the not-too-distant future, can be more empowering than conspiracy narratives alone because they often contain a strategy for preventing or reversing the corruption of society. When present in fiction, this can include protagonists whom extremist adherents may find relatable. In the case of *The Turner Diaries* and many of its imitators, the call for action is so specific that the novel doubles as an instructional manual.

Fiction is a particularly effective delivery mechanism for dystopian narratives, but it's not the only vehicle. Mainstream and extremist political rhetoric alike invoke the specter of current despair or near-future catastrophe on a regular basis and in a variety of formats, including speeches, articles, nonfiction books, and videos.[17]

Existential Threat

Extremists often describe threats to the continued existence of the in-group. Existential threats are usually perceived to be imminent, and they can take many forms, including military, cultural or racial.

Anti-Muslim extremists such as Anders Breivik frequently stipulate that Muslims present an existential threat to Western culture, stoking fears that Muslim immigration and proselytization will result in the complete overthrow of democracy and its replacement with an imagined "shariah law" theocracy.

Muslim extremists, such as American al Qaeda propagandist Anwar Awlaki, have argued the reverse proposition, that the West seeks to commit a comprehensive genocide against Muslims and Arabs. In a 2002 speech, Awlaki warned that Americans and Europeans "are going to approach all of the Arabs who are living in their midst, and every Arab man and woman and child will be killed. They will all be exterminated. A holocaust."[18]

The complete destruction of one's in-group is an intoxicating fear and an effective way to mobilize in-group members. When an extremist group escalates from oppressive crisis narratives (such as conspiracy and dystopia) into existential narratives (such as imminent genocide), it may signal that extremist violence will soon follow. However, some movements move to violence on the basis of lesser threats, while others perceive an existential threat positioned at some point in the distant future, which does not necessarily require a violent response now.

Apocalypse

The most advanced form of crisis narrative is apocalyptic—foretelling disaster not just for the in-group but for the world as we know it. Apocalyptic crisis narratives describe the end of history, often but not always in religious terms.

There are two types of apocalyptic narrative. The first simply describes the end of human society. Members of the in-group are urged to take action to prevent this catastrophe by opposing the apocalyptic actions of the out-group. For instance, the 2011 eco-extremist manifesto *Deep Green Resistance: Strategy to Save the Planet* argues that an out-group defined as "industrial civilization" or "industrial society" is wreaking environmental havoc that will lead to the destruction of "every living being" unless adherents fight back against the industrial system using sabotage and even violence.[19]

The second type of apocalyptic narrative is more insidious and seductive. A **millenarian belief** holds that the current world will be replaced by a perfect utopian world very soon. Millenarian apocalyptic movements believe that the end of the current age of history is fast approaching, a narrative typically predicated on prophecy. This climax brings a cosmic wave of destruction, usually related to an apocalyptic war between a chosen in-group and a demonic out-group, after which a perfect and utopian society will emerge.

Millenarian thought originated with Christian expectations that after Armageddon (a climactic battle between the forces of good and evil), Jesus will return to institute a thousand-year divine reign. Only after this period of human perfection will the world end and the final judgment ensue. In a millenarian context, an apocalyptic war is not simply an act of wanton destruction. It clears away the detritus of a dystopian temporal world in preparation for a perfect, utopian world to come.

Apocalyptic movements, sometimes short-lived but often consequential, have existed for millennia. Like conspiracy theories, they may be a response to uncertainty. British historian Norman Cohn, in his landmark study of medieval millenarians, wrote that such movements emerged during periods of "rapid economic and social change." The existence of static social roles created "a certain sense of security, a basic assurance which neither constant poverty nor occasional peril could destroy." When "traditional social bonds were being weakened or shattered," millenarian and apocalyptic movements were more likely to emerge.[20]

Triumphalism

Although current discourse around extremism is often founded on ideas about grievances and disadvantages, extremism does not exist only in populations that face genuine threats. We normally think of a crisis in terms of catastrophe, but the English word's root is derived from the Greek word *krisis*, "[the] act of separating, decision, judgment, event, outcome, turning point, sudden change." In English, as well, the word *crisis* can refer to an inflection point, a moment during which momentous action may change the course of history.[21]

A noncatastrophic crisis can emerge when an in-group experiences sudden and revolutionary success, particularly if that success is tied to successful hostile actions that damage or defeat an out-group. For extremist movements, this manifests as triumphalist rhetoric. Under this formulation, the crisis is not a challenge but an opportunity that requires adherents to engage actively in its full realization.

Perhaps the most infamous manifestation of this effect is *Triumph of the Will*, Leni Riefenstahl's 1935 Nazi propaganda epic filmed during an annual party rally, which showcases Adolf Hitler and the Nazi regime with displays of military and economic power alongside pomp and pageantry. While Nazism emerged from a period of turmoil and setbacks for the German people, it flourished under the glow of triumphalism.

Other extremist groups, notably Islamic State, have employed triumphalism to great effect. Al Qaeda built its propaganda and ideological platform on the premise that it employed terrorism because the movement was too weak to fight and win wars. Starting as early as 2011, the Islamic State in Iraq (which later became Islamic State) began to flip that narrative, using its propaganda to boast of strength and catalog successes. When Islamic State seized Mosul and declared itself a caliphate in June 2014, this provided a vindication of its triumphalist rhetoric and spurred the rapid growth of the organization into a global threat.

A blizzard of propaganda followed, emphasizing the historic nature of the caliphate and the allure of participation in a successful utopian project. These extremely successful messages created the illusion of a fully realized millenarian society that was perpetrating acts of extraordinary violence against Islamic State's many out-groups, especially Shia Muslims and Westerners.[22]

Triumphalist narratives focus on the maximum exaltation of the in-group (in this world, at least), but this exaltation is typically depicted as fragile. Only continued hostile action against the out-group can ensure the in-group's continued success. This out-group may or may not be referenced in triumphalist rhetoric, but its threat is never far from view.

Case Study: *The Protocols of the Learned Elders of Zion*

The infamous anti-Semitic conspiracy tract *The Protocols of the Learned Elders of Zion* has influenced a wide variety of extremist movements since its initial publication in 1903. The book was a semiplagiarized concatenation of conspiracy theories about Jewish influence over society, first published in Russian and later in English.[23] *Protocols* was published for an American audience in 1920 by Small, Maynard & Co. of Boston.[24]

Pushing a racial view of Jewish identity, *Protocols* has resonated throughout the years for many reasons, particularly because of its astute critique of modernity and representative government,[25] which was substantially stolen from Maurice Joly's 1864 book *Dialogue in Hell between Machiavelli and Montesquieu* (and other sources). In this French book, the salient critique is attributed to a fictionalized version of Niccolò Machiavelli in the context of the contemporaneous French emperor, Napoleon III.[26]

In *Protocols*, the critique is recast as a description of international crises caused by a race-based Jewish conspiracy. The crises are so diverse and wide-ranging that readers could readily associate them with worrisome developments in the real world. The prologue and appendix of the American edition frame the 1917 October Revolution of the Bolsheviks in Russia as a Jewish conspiracy, linking anti-Semitism to Communism, a conceit later adopted by a variety of extremist movements.

The conspiracy theories contained in *Protocols* were amplified and popularized by some of the biggest megaphones of the day, including the propaganda machine of Hitler and the Third Reich. Hundreds of articles based on *Protocols* were published in Henry Ford's newspaper, the *Dearborn Independent,* helping to popularize anti-Semitism in the United States.[27]

The *Protocols* conspiracy theory played a critical part in the evolution of the relatively low-key British Israelist identity movement (chapter 3) into Christian Identity, a virulent and violent racist religion. As British Israelist authors were exposed to *Protocols*, it shifted their perception of Jewish identity from a close alignment with Anglo-Saxony to deadly enmity.

In one particularly notable text, a pseudonymous British Israelist writer conflated the *Protocols* conspiracy theory with the format of a dystopian novel and a Christian millenarian vision to create the first formal statement of Christian Identity. Published in 1944, *When? A Prophetical Novel of the Very Near Future* melded the *Protocols* conspiracy with British Israelist scriptural precedents to suggest that Jews were literally the genetic descendants of Satan, an argument that was taken up more forcefully by subsequent writers. The novel presented this conspiracy as the proximate cause of World War III, which concludes with the arrival of Christ on Earth to separate the races and establish a millenarian reign.[28]

Today, the *Protocols* conspiracy is influential in a wide range of extremist movements, usually in its original anti-Semitic context but sometimes in vague language describing an out-group of "globalists" and "bankers."[29] The *Protocols* conspiracy theory has also spread widely in the Arab world,[30] including in media and ideological circles connected to Hezbollah and Hamas.[31]

Solutions

The existence of a crisis demands an urgent response, a solution to whatever challenge the crisis presents. Extremism's **crisis-solution construct** posits that a crisis affecting the in-group has been caused by an out-group or -groups, and that the crisis can only be resolved by taking hostile action against the out-group. This construct is at the core of extremist ideology and propaganda, creating what Haroro J. Ingram, a leading scholar of nonstate violent actors' propaganda, calls a "system of meaning"—an extremist in-group's "alternative perspective of the world" that stands in contrast to the views of both out-groups and (in most cases) the eligible in-group.[32]

This alternative view is constructed from the elements of extremist belief—identity, crisis, and solution—to justify extraordinary measures. To protect the eligible in-group from the crisis caused by the out-group, the extremist in-group proposes solutions that reflect the magnitude of the threat it has described, without necessarily being proportionate.

The most common solutions proposed by extremist movements are:

• **Harassment:** Intentionally making out-groups unwelcome in the presence of the in-group

- **Discrimination:** Denying out-group members benefits provided to in-group members

- **Segregation:** Physical separation of the in-group from out-groups

- **Hate crimes:** Nonsystematic violence against out-group members

- **Terrorism:** Public violence targeting noncombatants to advance an extremist ideology

- **Oppression:** Aggressive and systematic discrimination, up to and including systematic violence

- **War:** Open lethal fighting between an in-group and an out-group

- **Genocide:** Systematic slaughter of out-group members on a large scale.

Harassment

Harassment can include verbal abuse, intentional offense, or incursions into out-group personal or shared spaces that fall short of violence (such as vandalism). Harassment is one of the earliest and most common elements of extremist action, and it often forebodes greater radicalization. At minimum, harassment reinforces in-group cohesion and reinforces the low status of out-group members. At its worst, harassment can be used systematically to inflict psychological harm or intimidate out-groups and discourage them from participating in civic affairs or using public facilities. When harassment escalates in intensity, or becomes an element of in-group cohesion (for instance, when the use of a racial epithet becomes an in-group identity marker), violence may not be far behind.

Discrimination

Discrimination can be a product of nonideological hostility or systemic bias toward an out-group rather than a deliberate strategy. At an organic level, dislike, distrust, or legacy social and economic structures can lead to discriminatory behavior that excludes the out-group from the privileges or social circles of the in-group (for instance, in employment, education, and housing opportunities).

Discrimination can also be a deliberate strategy. Many Islamist movements explicitly deny certain rights to non-Muslims as part of their governing structure.[33] In other cases, discrimination may be intentional but covert. For example, U.S. President Richard Nixon reportedly pursued specific antidrug policies as a way to target African Americans without doing so explicitly.[34]

The endorsement of intentionally discriminatory behavior qualifies a movement as extremist under the definition used in this book. Some forms of systemic discrimination arguably fall into a gray area, although at times they reflect the presence of extremist currents in society.

Systemic discrimination also can be a legacy of prior extremist policies that have been incompletely mitigated. For example, in addition to more current factors, generations of slavery, legal discrimination and disenfranchisement have created significant structural obstacles to the creation of wealth in African American communities.[35]

Segregation

Segregation ranges from the creation of physical barriers between the in-group and out-group to the relocation of in-groups and out-groups into separate territories. Examples include the former Jim Crow laws in the United States and current white separatist movements such as the Northwest Territorial Imperative, which encourages whites to migrate to the Pacific Northwest and establish ethnic enclaves.[36] Segregation may be notionally voluntary, but it is rarely nonviolent in the long term because sooner or later it must be enforced.

Ethnic cleansing, the term for forcibly segregating a territory by expelling out-groups, is typically extremely violent. Minorities are usually incentivized to leave territories controlled by the in-group through massacres and violent intimidation, which is why ethnic cleansing campaigns are often rightly classified as genocide.

Hate Crimes

A hate crime—the targeting of people for violence or criminal harassment based on race, religion, gender, sexual identity, or other identity—can be one manifestation of ideological extremism. However, law enforcement and other public data on hate crimes is often inadequate to assess fully. Some so-called hate crimes are certainly driven by extremist beliefs, such as Dylann Roof's 2015 murder of nine people in a Charleston, South Carolina, church and should properly be classified as terrorism because the goal was to send a political message. But not all extremists leave behind manifestos, as Roof did. Often, bigotry arises in people without a clearly defined extremist ideology, and that bigotry can lead to violence. Additional quantitative and qualitative research is urgently needed to help identify why people commit hate crimes and how many of those people have been exposed to an extremist ideology. But although some hate crimes may not be extremist, some certainly are, and hate crimes are one form of violent solution that extremist ideologies may endorse.[37]

Terrorism

Because extremist movements are often small, some adopt the asymmetric tactic of terrorism, which allows relatively weak movements to have a disproportionate impact on large and powerful out-groups. In the twentieth and twenty-first centuries, rapid advances in technology boosted the capacity for cost-effective mass killing and social disruption by smaller groups and individuals, elevating the threat and frequency of terrorism accordingly.[38]

Terrorism is defined here as "public violence targeting noncombatants, carried out by nongovernmental individuals or groups, in order to advance a political or ideological goal or amplify a political or ideological message."[39] When carried out by a governmental actor, I would call similar public violence *oppression* (see the next section) rather than terrorism.

Terrorism serves multiple purposes for an extremist group, including the mobilization of supporters and sympathizers, as well as creating friction between an eligible in-group and an out-group, contributing to the radicalization of both groups.

Islamic State and its precursor group, al Qaeda in Iraq, have been particularly successful at using terrorism to radicalize all parties in a conflict. In 2006, al Qaeda in Iraq bombed a Shia mosque in Samarra, triggering a wave of sectarian reprisals between Shia and Sunni Muslims that left thousands dead. The attack set the stage for a much wider conflict by engaging more of the Sunni eligible in-group with the extremist in-group and encouraging the escalation of existing extremist currents among Iraq's Shia population and politicians.[40] Subsequent iterations of the terrorist organization repeatedly struck against existing social fracture lines in an effort to reproduce this success.[41]

Extremist terrorism usually targets out-groups, but it can also target ineligible in-group members, or even eligible in-group members. One notable example of this was the 2011 Norway attack by Anders Breivik, who killed seventy-seven people in Norway, the vast majority of whom were Norwegians (his own in-group) at a youth summer camp, in order to send a message about the threat he constructed as emanating from Muslim out-groups.[42] The primary purpose of terrorism is to spread an ideological message, and the identity of the victims may be secondary or tertiary to perpetrators. Although some ideologies prohibit violence against in-group members, targeting tactics tend to be very fluid, especially concerning ineligible in-group members who are seen as apostates, collaborators, or traitors.

Oppression

Oppression typically includes heightened forms of discrimination and segregation, such as racial slavery, internment camps, and other drastic curtailment of rights for members of out-groups. Oppression almost always includes an explicit legal framework mandating hostile action against an out-group. Examples include the Spanish Inquisition, the internment of Japanese Americans during World War II, the Islamic State's enslavement of the

Yazidi minority group, and more generally, the imprisonment of people on the basis of their identity group, such as race, religion, sexual orientation, or sexual identity.

War and Insurgency

The history of humanity is littered with wars, some more closely related to extremism than others. As previously noted, conflict and war are not automatically extremist. But many wars and insurgencies (including both World War I and World War II) are tied closely to extremist actions and movements in one way or another (as noted in chapter 1). More recently, a number of wars in the post-9/11 era have been launched with the stated goal of defeating extremism, including the U.S.-led invasions of Afghanistan and Iraq. Instead, these efforts have created conditions under which extremism can thrive, including jihadist insurgencies in both countries and related conflicts involving al Qaeda and Islamic State in Mali, Nigeria, the Philippines, Somalia, and Yemen. War and insurgency can empower extremist movements, even when the extremists cannot manage a clean win.

Genocide

Nazi documents of the 1940s euphemistically referred to the "Final Solution of the Jewish Question," using bureaucratic language to describe the ugly concept of genocide.[43] This final solution is found at the conclusion of the radicalization process if it is carried through to its fullest realization. If an out-group is stipulated to represent an eternal and existential threat to the in-group and if the solution to that threat is inseparable from violence, then an extremist ideology can escalate until the only remaining solution is the complete and permanent annihilation of the out-group.

For most extremist groups, genocide remains largely notional. White nationalist readers of the novel *The Turner Diaries*, for instance, envision genocide as a long-term goal but their own direct actions as incremental. Adherents do not seek to implement genocide in real time but rather intend to spark a race war that will theoretically create the conditions for genocide at some future date.[44]

But some extremist movements do attempt to implement total genocide in real time, and some succeed. As discussed in chapter 1, the Roman Catholic Church successfully exterminated the Cathar sect during the Albigensian crusade in the thirteenth century. A series of global genocides have nearly or totally wiped out indigenous peoples in the Americas, Australia, the Caucasus, Tasmania, and other regions.[45] Other genocides have been stopped before they could succeed in exterminating the out-group but still produced casualties ranging from thousands to millions. In addition to the genocide of 6 million Jews, the Nazis killed millions of other civilians on the basis of ethnicity, disability or sexual identity.[46]

Genocide is the end of the road for radicalization into extremism, a process this book has defined as the escalation of an in-group's extremist orientation in the form of increasingly negative views about an out-group or the endorsement of increasingly hostile or violent actions against an out-group. But not every extremist movement travels the entire way down the road to reach this final destination. Understanding the process by which groups and individuals do or do not radicalize can shed light on why extremism presents such an enduring problem in human history and how we can work to reduce its toll on society.

Case Study: *The Spook Who Sat by the Door*

An example of how extremists pair crises and solutions can be found in *The Spook Who Sat by the Door*,[47] a 1969 black nationalist novel by African American writer Sam Greenlee.[48] Greenlee was a military veteran and former government propagandist. His novel tells the story of Dan Freeman, the first black agent with the U.S. Central Intelligence Agency (CIA), who takes his professional training to the streets to lead a black revolution.

Freeman is recruited as a token minority agent to address a politically inspired controversy over the agency's lack of racial integration. He is placed in a highly visible post with little responsibility. The title of the book is a play on words referring to his job (to sit by the door and be seen), with the word *spook* as double-entendre—in one context as a slang term for *spy* and in a different context as a racial epithet.

The book presents a dystopian crisis in which white Americans are universally aligned against black Americans, with even seeming allies betraying a racist agenda in private moments. The crisis in *The Spook Who Sat by the Door* is embellished but not extensively. It is reflective of the genuine civil rights struggles of the book's era. However, its unyielding insistence that white Americans are universally incapable of sincere good will toward blacks situates it firmly in an extremist worldview.

Freeman takes the CIA job in order to receive training in violent covert action tactics, using his position to study global insurgencies, with the intention of taking that knowledge back to the poor Chicago neighborhoods where he grew up. Freeman seeds and guides a black insurgency by recruiting and training gang members, whom he organizes into covert cells in several major cities. Attacks that create economic pressure are key to the strategy, in this case with the intent of making white politicians choose between maintaining racist policies and maintaining the United States as a global superpower.

The insurgents rob banks to fund their operations and rob armories to gain access to munitions in preparation for revolution. The book follows the insurgency through its successful launch against the backdrop of riots in Chicago. The use of violence in *Spook* is framed as necessary, justified, and inevitable, but it is also predicated on provocation. The book ends in the middle of its protagonists' revolution, but its stated goal is the destruction of the existing white-dominated economic and political system.

The book describes the revolutionaries' tactics in detail, advancing militant black nationalism as a solution to the crisis of racism, with plenty of specific suggestions. As Freeman teaches tactics to the gang members he has recruited, he also teaches readers. In a 2003 interview, Greenlee said that the book was intended to be "a training manual for guerilla warfare. That's why it scared the white folks so much."[49]

The book was adapted as a movie amid some controversy in 1973, roughly a year before white nationalist William Luther Pierce began work on *The Turner Diaries*, an infamous racist dystopian novel that contains similar instructional material and helped inspire the Oklahoma City bombing in 1995. *The Turner Diaries* outlines a dystopian crisis informed by conspiracy theories, including *The Protocols of the Learned Elders of Zion*, and proposes a solution that includes terrorism and culminates in a global genocide against all nonwhite races.

The race-obsessed Pierce may have noticed the controversy surrounding the film, which was abruptly pulled from U.S. movie theaters (a move that Greenlee attributed to the Federal Bureau of Investigation's dirty tricks),[50] but he was also reportedly inspired by a similar antigovernment novel, *The John Franklin Letters*, published in 1959.[51] Fictional works such as these provide a particularly vivid window into how extremist narratives are shaped into a crisis-solution construct that urges potential adherents to mobilize toward violence.

The Extremist Equation

This book has defined extremism as the belief that an in-group's success or survival can never be separated from the need for hostile action against an out-group. When the completed identity construct meets the crisis-solution construct, all of these elements fall into place and create the potential for the in-group to escalate its demands for legitimacy—the process of radicalization, in which views of the out-group become increasingly negative and the range of obligatory hostile actions against the out-group grows more severe.

Each component is part of a broader testimony to the cohesion and historicity of both the in-group and the out-group, with the former portrayed in a positive light and the latter in a negative light. These narratives set the stage for understanding the out-group as a negative force in the world.

The added complication of a crisis narrative positions the out-group as an intrinsic threat to in-group legitimacy, from minor threats (such as diluting in-group purity) to major threats (such as participating in an apocalyptic scenario). The adoption of necessary solutions—in the form of hostile actions against the out-group—completes the extremist equation.

RADICALIZATION

Why do people and groups embrace extremism? Decades of research have failed to answer this question definitively, or more accurately, decades of research have carefully eliminated many proposed explanations.

Although many assumptions about drivers of radicalization have been disproven, policymakers and politicians cling to them nonetheless, as do people working to fight extremism on the front lines of communities where it thrives.

One of the most repeated assertions is that extremism results from structural development factors, such as poverty, high unemployment, or lack of educational opportunity. This assertion is intuitively attractive to some policymakers, in part because they have experience trying to solve structural problems and in part because such explanations soothe their anxieties about the human condition.[1]

But the role of structural factors has been repeatedly discredited. A study of terrorist attacks from 1986 to 2002 found no correlation between low gross domestic product and incidence of terrorism, a finding that has been replicated again and again across different measures and time frames.[2]

Two 2016 studies based on Islamic State foreign fighter data deeply undercut structural explanations for the group's success. One found that countries with higher economic prosperity and lower inequality were *more* likely than countries without these conditions to see residents travel to Syria as foreign fighters and that unemployment was "not highly correlated" to overall foreign fighter activity.[3] The other reported similar findings, noting that correlations with structural factors did appear in some places but not others. Taken as a whole across all geographic regions, the data did not support generalizations about structural development factors as drivers of extremism.[4]

Regarding education, a correlation exists but not the one you might think. A study of more than four thousand jihadist radicals found that their average education level was considerably higher than the general population.[5] In a study of Palestinian terrorism, researchers found that higher levels of both education and economic achievement positively correlated with membership in Hamas and Palestinian Islamic Jihad.[6] Despite these findings, no one advocates for reducing educational opportunities as a way to counter violent extremism.

Correlations to lower education or standard of living can be found inconsistently in very constrained social contexts and in geographically limited settings. One large-scale study found a correlation between high unemployment and high foreign fighter flows from within the Muslim world but found the opposite correlation for foreign fighters from non-Muslim countries. It should be noted that the "Muslim world" dataset included failed states and countries beset by civil wars and insurgencies. There are obvious risks in arguing for single-issue causation in settings where multiple variables may apply.[7]

Generally speaking, any given argument for structural causes looks better when the sample size is smaller. For instance, unemployment correlates for some cities and countries in smaller-scale studies, especially at the level of troubled neighborhoods like Belgium's Molenbeek[8] or Somali communities in Minneapolis. But neighborhoods that have an unemployment problem may not be more prone to produce violent extremists. They may simply produce violent extremists with an unemployment problem.

Billions of people around the world face problems in their personal lives and in their communities—injustice, oppression, discrimination, poverty, unemployment, crime, and more. But only a small fraction of people with problems take up extremism.

Another popular and corrosive assumption is that extremism is primarily caused by religion in general or by one religion specifically. Chapters 1 and 2 of this book document the fact that extremism is not simply a product of religious belief, nor is it confined to any one religion. Religion matters to religious extremists in the same way that race matters to racial extremists—as their particular in-group identity.

The tenets of any religion can be bent to the service of radicalization and used to fill in the contents of an ideology, even when key passages argue against violence. Christian extremists have flourished throughout history despite Jesus's famous instruction to his disciples to turn the other cheek when they were attacked. Buddhists—renowned for nonviolence in the popular imagination—have also been involved in extremism, both historically, as when sixteenth-century Mongol rulers violently imposed Buddhism as the state religion,[9] and in contemporary conflicts in Sri Lanka and in Myanmar.[10]

That fact that religion is not a proximate cause of extremism is not a reason to avoid studying how religion informs extremism. For religious extremists, scriptures and beliefs are sources of information that are used to define in-group and out-group identities. Understanding the details of extremist religious belief can help us understand how extremist in-groups seek to recruit from eligible in-groups, and it can help us predict specific actions that a religious extremist movement might take. But we cannot attribute extremism to religious belief without excluding or misconstruing some of the most dramatic and destructive examples in history.

The desire for simple explanations keeps many of these incorrect assumptions alive. But to understand why people become extremists and how to combat extremist violence, we must move past the old clichés and find something better.

Individuals and Groups

Discussions about extremism sometimes gloss over the differences between individual radicalization and group radicalization. Although they are closely related, these are distinct processes. With the exception of wholly original ideologues—the 0.0001 percent of the 0.01 percent of people who become violent extremists—group radicalization precedes individual radicalization.

Only in extraordinarily rare cases, such as the Unabomber, can individual extremist action be separated from a clear association with a preexisting movement. Even in that case, Ted Kaczynski drew on previous works and ideas, although his concatenation was fairly unique. Kaczynski also influenced other extremists, including Norwegian

Group radicalization precedes individual radicalization.

mass-murderer Anders Breivik, who plagiarized the Una-bomber's manifesto in his own.[11]

Although radicalization almost always involves the adoption of a specific ideology, the process of adoption is more instructive than the contents of the ideology. When the study of radicalization as a process becomes fixated on contents, the results are a bewildering mess that distorts analytical efforts. A content-driven approach produces a menagerie of competing theories that make sense only in the context of a single movement at a single point in time, such as arguments that extremism is caused by colo-nialism or religious fundamentalism.[12] When these theo-ries are applied to other movements—even very similar movements—they often fail.

The models discussed below are therefore presented at a very high level of abstraction. But at the same time, they describe concrete criteria that can be applied to specific cases as well as to strategies for countering extremism.

The group radicalization framework presented here was derived from the study of propaganda and ideological texts produced by the white nationalist movement Chris-tian Identity, al Qaeda, and Islamic State.[13] The individual radicalization framework is derived from the study of on-line recruitment and behaviors for white nationalists and jihadists.[14]

It should be noted that the development and deploy-ment of extremist ideologies are abstracted here, but they are not entirely abstract. Individual ideologues and extremist leaders deploy these frameworks for a variety of reasons, and they possess intangible qualities, such as charisma, that may help advance their arguments.[15] For some, this may be a cynical exercise in power-seeking. Within Islamic State, for instance, some leaders were true believers, and others were simply exploiting social dynamics.[16] Extremism is frequently a minority enterprise, even if leaders believe it will bring them power.

Osama bin Laden threw away his wealth and status to live in hiding and fight a hopeless jihad. It is difficult to imagine that he acted out of any conventional power-seeking motive. For others, such as Adolf Hitler, it is unclear where the desire for power ended and true belief in Nazi ideals began, but the truth almost certainly lay somewhere between those poles.[17] In contrast, the demonization and subsequent extermination of the Cathars by a series of Roman Catholic popes in the eleventh century was driven by a number of purely secular and political considerations, although some element of belief came into play.[18]

The process of becoming an ideologue or believer and the process of leading or joining a group of extremists are ultimately individual journeys, with almost as many variations as there are participants. But that journey almost always falls within a unifying social framework of ideas and texts that we can understand and apply. As Hannah Arendt writes, citing Plato, political entities "do not spring from oak and rock," but neither do they "spring from within our particular and individual selves."[19]

Group Radicalization

The preceding chapters define the elements of group radicalization as a series of postulates that we can place in a rough sequence. Not every extremist movement will pass through these stages in exactly the same order. But in order to qualify as extremist using the definition in this book, a movement must take the following steps:

1. *Define the in-group:* Before a movement becomes extremist, some sort of in-group must be defined. This definition can be detailed or vague, but some kind of in-group collective identity is required in order for a movement to cohere.

2. *Define an out-group:* In-group members can be avid, devout, patriotic, and even fanatical without becoming extremists. In order to progress into extremism, an out-group must be defined clearly and in some detail. For some extremist movements, the ineligible in-group can be substituted for a formal out-group.

3. *Define the existence of the out-group as an acute crisis for the in-group:* An out-group description—even an unfriendly one—is not enough to vault a movement into extremism. The out-group's identity must be seen as an intrinsic obstacle or threat to the health of the in-group, precipitating a crisis. The crisis cannot be temporary, conditional, or amenable to settlement. It must be perceived as inseparable from the existence of the out-group.

4. *Define hostile actions (solutions) that must be applied to the out-group:* By definition, a crisis requires a decisive response. After a crisis has been stipulated, the in-group must settle on a course of hostile action toward the out-group in order for a movement to be placed on the extremist spectrum.

These four conditions place a movement on the extremist spectrum. Once on the spectrum, a movement can radicalize (by adopting increasingly negative views about the out-group and endorsing increasingly hostile action), or it can moderate (by mitigating its views of the out-group or shifting to a lower scale of hostile action, such as abandoning an ideological commitment to genocide in favor of segregation). As a noun, the word *moderate* implies a nonextremist orientation, but as a verb, it denotes movement to a less extreme orientation. Extremist groups can "moderate" without becoming "moderates."

After these four conditions are in place, an extremist movement must flesh out each category of description by linking it to sources of information, including historical information, scriptures and prophecy, news (real and fake), analysis, and conspiracy theories. As these details are filled in, a movement's identity construction becomes more robust. As more negative information is collected about the out-group, the scale of the crisis becomes more extreme, and the prescribed solution becomes more violent.

As the process of radicalization proceeds, the identity construct is paired with the crisis-solution construct to create the extremist value proposition:

1. A crisis is caused by the out-group, which afflicts the eligible in-group.

2. The eligible in-group can resolve the crisis only by joining the extremist in-group's hostile action against the out-group.

Individual Radicalization

The study of extremist recruitment practices suggests that individual radicalization is similar to any process of political mobilization but with an emphasis on identity and on crisis-solution constructs.[20] An individual who becomes

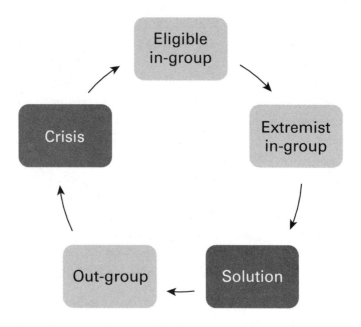

Figure 3 The extremist value proposition

radicalized will usually pass through the following stages, not necessarily in this order:

1. *Identification with the (eligible) in-group:* Prior to radicalization, individuals come to associate themselves with a mainstream identity, such as black, Latinx, white, Buddhist, Christian, Jewish, Muslim, or any other.

2. *Negative views toward an out-group:* Individuals develop negative views about an out-group or -groups based on

their intrinsic identity rather than a short-term conflict. This stage may precede or follow the perception of a crisis or curiosity about an extremist movement.

3. *Perception of crisis:* Individuals come to believe that a crisis is affecting the eligible in-group. The initial perception of a crisis may or may not attribute the crisis to negative views about an out-group.

4. *Curiosity about the extremist in-group:* Individuals learn of the existence of an extremist movement and seek more information about its ideology, either by reading texts or by making direct contact with adherents. Individuals may become curious about an extremist in-group before developing negative views of an out-group or a perception of crisis.

5. *Consideration of the extremist in-group:* Individuals review what they have learned about the extremist ideology and its adherents and evaluate the pros and cons of further engagement. The most important question at this juncture is whether the individual concludes that the extremist in-group offers a genuine solution to the eligible in-group crisis. Significant numbers of people pass through the first four stages, but at this stage, the field starts to winnow out, and far fewer will proceed to each subsequent stage.

6. *Identification with the extremist in-group:* Individuals begin to think of themselves as aligned with or as adherents

of the extremist ideology, agreeing that the extremist in-group offers a solution to the crisis. Direct contact with other adherents of the extremist in-group may or may not occur.

7. *Self-critique:* Individuals ask themselves whether their actions in support of the eligible in-group or the extremist in-group are an adequate response to the crisis. If the answer is yes, individuals will maintain their identification at the current level. If the answer is no, individuals may decide to escalate their involvement with the extremist movement. The self-critique is repeated periodically with the potential for additional escalation.

8. *Escalation:* Individuals who determine that they are not adequately responding to the crisis may escalate their actions on behalf of the extremist in-group, including an increased risk that they will engage in hostile actions against an out-group (such as hate crimes, terrorist attacks, or foreign fighting).

9. *After-action critique:* Individuals will evaluate the impact of their escalated involvement in terms of tangible and intangible benefits to themselves and to the group. Depending on the result of this critique, the individual may opt to escalate further, deescalate by reconsidering the extremist ideology, or continue at the current level.

Some people take years to go through the process of radicalization, from its initial stages to the decision to act; others speed through it in months or even weeks. Some individuals will leapfrog past certain steps. So-called lone wolf terrorists may skip some of these steps entirely. However, if people carry out lone-wolf-style attacks without having significantly engaged with this radicalization process, we should question whether they should be properly understood as extremist adherents or as pathological mass killers. Members of the latter category may loosely invoke an extremist movement they have not meaningfully engaged with.

Grievances

One element that runs through both the ideological narratives of extremism and the expressed beliefs of individuals who have been radicalized is the idea of grievance. Grievances are a common element in extremist arguments and rationalizations, to such an extent that some models of radicalization include the adoption of grievances as a necessary element of extremism.[21] Others argue that specific legitimate grievances cited by extremists—such as colonialism or oppression—are the proximate causes of extremism and terrorism.[22]

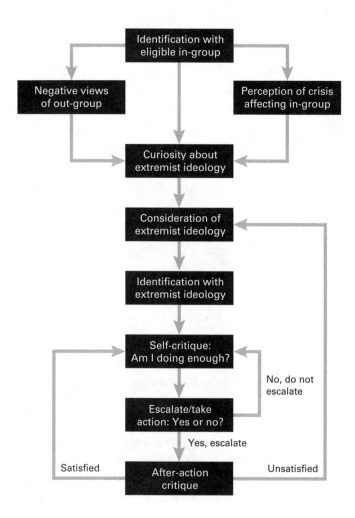

Figure 4 The individual radicalization process

But as noted at the beginning of this chapter, grievances (legitimate or not) do not always lead to extremism. All extremists have grievances, but not all people with grievances become extremists. When grievances appear in extremist ideologies, they are often generalized and always framed in the context of a crisis (chapter 4).

Specific grievances do appear to play a role in mobilizing people toward violence—in this radicalization model, the stages of self-critique and decision to act. A study of 115 mass murders found that the only significant predictor of violence was "the presence of a grievance, specifically a grievance against a person or entity, as opposed to a grievance against a category of people or a grievance against an idea, movement or religion."[23] Grievance is defined here as "the cause of the offender's distress or resentment, a perception of having been treated unfairly or inappropriately." The study was not limited to ideological or extremist murders, although specific grievances against individuals or entities often come into play in such cases.

Identity and crisis-solution construction lay out a broad framework within which individual grievances can be contextualized as part of a sweeping identity-based conflict. This dynamic can be seen in many cases of extremist violence. For instance, Oklahoma City bomber Timothy McVeigh was exposed to *The Turner Diaries* (chapter 4) during the late 1980s and subsequently developed significant antigovernment views. But he was mobilized to violence by a specific event—the FBI's botched raid on a cult compound in Waco, Texas, that left seventy-six people dead.[24]

Many recent jihadists were similarly mobilized by the Syrian regime's brutal attacks on its own people, which they obsessively analyzed in specific detail through a barrage of brutal videos disseminated over social media.[25]

Key to the definition of grievance is the idea that it "is more than a momentary feeling of discontent or a short-lived, even explosive, expression of anger or frustration; rather, it is a conclusion reached about the reason for the offender's suffering (or the suffering of others about whom the offender cares)": it is "a function of concreteness—a tangible, identifiable object to which causation of suffering can be ascribed."[26]

Extremist ideologies promote the legitimacy of the in-group as a collective, expanding the circle of people that adherents care about by affirming in-group identity as so robust and important that the suffering of one member must be contextualized as part of the suffering of all members. Secondarily, they argue that the out-group is the concrete cause of the in-group's suffering, making this argument tangible through a lengthy descriptive process. Finally, extremist ideologies and propaganda point to out-group targets for violence or other hostile action, with varying levels of specificity, stipulating that the hostile action will (ultimately) ease the suffering of the in-group.

In essence, extremist ideologies weld grievances to a system of meaning in which they become both universal and personal, while insisting on hostile action to resolve the conflict. This toxic worldview can then be applied to help mobilize hostile action against specific individuals or entities associated with an out-group. In this sense, grievances and radicalization should probably understood as co-dependent or enabling, rather than a linear causation. More research on this dynamic would almost certainly produce fruitful insights.

Why Radicalization Happens

Each of the models above shows *how* people and groups can escalate into extremism and then into violent extremism, but they don't illustrate *why*. As the opening of this chapter suggests, the question of why people turn to extremism has been studied at great length, but many of the explanations proffered are flawed. In some cases, the evidence directly contradicts the proposed theories of why radicalization happens. In other cases, the explanations make sense only when the study is limited by ideology, chronology, geography, or all of the above.

Most of us have experienced the daunting challenge of explaining how any one human being makes decisions and develops beliefs. Sometimes we can't even explain how we arrived at our own beliefs, so we should not expect that we can make absolute conclusions about the behavior and beliefs of other individuals and groups.

Although we can't consistently predict behavior, we can identify tendencies that reflect various social and psychological factors that inform outcomes. Sometimes we can identify the tendency more definitively than we can explain it.

The complexity of this topic precludes a comprehensive treatment here, but two potential drivers of radicalization are supported by research and are applicable across ideological boundaries: the effects of categorization and learning bias, and the effects of disruptions to the status quo.

Categorization and Learning Bias

As is discussed in chapter 3, categorization takes place when an individual adopts a collective identity. A number of experimental and research studies have demonstrated that simply understanding oneself to be part of an in-group correlates with a tendency toward discrimination or hostility against out-groups.

This does not necessarily apply in every context. For instance, groups that were placed in competitive settings developed negative attitudes about out-groups much more strongly than groups that were placed in cooperative settings. But groups that were placed in a neutral context also developed negative attitudes toward out-groups, suggesting that the tendency to develop negative attitudes about out-groups is—to some extent—hardwired, either in the minds of individuals or as a necessary byproduct of many contexts in which we interact socially.[27]

The systematic construction of an identity narrative, which is seen in some mainstream groups and is very pronounced in extremist groups, exploits this tendency to develop prejudice against out-groups. An extremist ideology's detailed descriptions of in-groups and out-groups creates prototypes for each group, which then become stereotypes when generalized. The qualities of prototypes—"attitudes, beliefs, values and behaviors"[28]—closely track with the identity definitions described in this book, which were derived from extremist ideological texts. As social psychologist Michael A. Hogg writes:

> When we categorize someone as a member of a group we assign the group's prototypical attributes to that person, and view them through the lens of the prototype; seeing them not as unique individuals but as more or less prototypical group members—a process called depersonalization.[29]

The accumulation of negative data points is enhanced by learning bias. When people have negative perceptions about something they encounter (as with out-groups), they may tend to avoid further contact with it, which inhibits them from encountering new information that might correct their negative perception.[30] For extremist movements, barriers to corrective information are institutionalized when the ideology radicalizes to the point that it urges in-group members to avoid contact with the out-group.

Disruptions to the Status Quo

The second major factor that helps tilt people toward extremism is uncertainty. People have a tendency to prefer the status quo. Psychology scholars John T. Jost and Roderick M. Kramer argue that

> people tend to use ideas about groups and individuals to justify the way things are, so that existing social arrangements are perceived as fair and legitimate, perhaps even natural and inevitable.[31]

People have a general cognitive bias toward seeing the status quo as just and fair.[32] Biases in favor of the status quo may arise for any number of reasons, including a desire to rationalize one's current experience of life, systemic rewards for accepting the status quo (such as social and economic success), and the reduction of uncertainty and anxiety. Studies suggest the tendency to prefer the status quo is strong enough to overcome biases against out-groups, even when the status quo disadvantages one's own group and provides advantages to a competing group.[33] Thus, a stable status quo serves as a bulwark against radicalization.

When the status quo is overturned, people become uncertain—about their safety, their livelihoods, and their places in the world and society. The status quo can be disrupted in endless ways—including economic, technological, political, military, and social change. War, for instance, can cause great uncertainty, especially civil wars in which former friends and neighbors may suddenly become enemy combatants. Wars can cause people to relocate away from an area dominated by their in-group and into an area dominated by a different identity collective that considers them an out-group.

Revolutions in communications technology may create new opportunities for intergroup social contact or new arenas for intergroup conflict. A wave of immigration can change the demographics—and even the definition—of a national in-group, affecting the definition of pre-existing overlapping group identities, such as race or religion.

On an individual level, deep personal trauma, such as job loss or the death of a loved one, can also cause uncertainty, and this is reflected in the biographies of many lone wolf extremists and other kinds of mass killers.[34] Another clue can be found in religious terrorism, particularly jihadism, where religious converts are often disproportionately represented. In some cases, people who adopt religious extremism are drawn to exploring alternative religious identities due to fundamental questions about themselves and their place in the world.[35]

Seismic shifts erode the boundaries and definitions of in-groups and out-groups, especially when people are being physically, economically, or socially displaced. Because people tend to see the status quo as just, these dramatic changes may be perceived as unjust, overturning norms that are perceived mostly as fair and right.[36]

Uncertainty is uncomfortable and produces anxiety until it can be resolved. Most people deal with uncertainty in healthy ways, but many do not—enough to make a statistical difference. Although there are a number of ways people act to reduce uncertainty in their lives, one very effective strategy is to adopt a group identity that is "distinctive and clearly defined," according to Michael A. Hogg, head of the social psychology program at Claremont Graduate University and the creator of uncertainty-identity theory, which seeks to describe the connection between uncertainty and extremism.[37]

At low levels, uncertainty can spur positive excitement and productive behavior, as when people are presented with a problem or challenge they think they can solve. But when people are presented with problems or threats that they think they cannot solve—because the problem is too

When people are presented with problems or threats that they think they cannot solve—because the problem is too big or because they lack the necessary resources to address it—they can adopt negative behaviors.

big or because they lack the necessary resources to address it—they can adopt negative behaviors.[38]

In addition to its strong empirical support, the uncertainty frame has the benefit of possibly redeeming some of the disproven structural arguments highlighted at the start of this chapter. For example, poverty or unemployment may not be linked to terrorism, but sudden disruptive changes in an economic environment might create uncertainty that exacerbates in-group and out-group tensions.

People may experience uncertainty when faced with changing demographics or the introduction of new technologies. Weak states, insurgencies, and civil war create high levels of uncertainty because they divide in-groups, create new out-groups, and often defy clean resolutions. Additional historical study may shed light on these questions and help illuminate the conditions under which extremism thrives.

Why Extremist Ideology Works

The elements of extremism outlined in chapters 3 and 4 are derived from the close study of extremist ideological texts. These elements intersect with the psychological needs identified by uncertainty-identity theory.

Extremist ideologies meet the need for certainty by providing a quality known as *entitativity*, defined as "the property of a group, resting on clear boundaries, internal homogeneity, social interaction, clear internal structure, common goals, and common fate."[39] All of these characteristics contribute to making groups feel authentic and real, and most of them are explicitly addressed by extremist ideologies. Entitativity is cultivated by extremist ideologues using the following tools:

• **Clear boundaries and internal homogeneity:** As is noted in chapter 3, extremist ideologies provide extremely clear, rigid rules that define who is part of the in-group, who is part of the out-group, and under what circumstances members of the eligible in-group risk assignment to an out-group. This contrasts with nonextremist identities, in which the boundaries between in-group and out-group are more negotiable and less emphasized.

• **Common goals and a common fate:** Extremist ideologies invest significantly in defining the past, present, and future practices of both the in-group and the out-group, typically in an interconnected narrative that concludes with a final confrontation. Extremist groups may define expectations for the future in more specific detail than nonextremist movements do. They also tend to project their expectations into a compressed timeline, closer to imminent than distant.[40] Practices are arguably the most important element in an extremist identity definition. Although we might dislike out-group members for what they believe or because of their traits, it is far easier to frame a crisis and mobilize action based on what they do.

• **Social interaction:** Extremist ideologies outline the rules for social interaction, including an obligation to support and protect fellow in-group members and strict rules governing contact with the out-group. Friendly contact with the out-group is typically proscribed, and hostile contact is encouraged.

• **Clear internal structure:** This varies substantially from group to group. State-based extremists are able to offer the most well-defined social structures, whereas nonstate extremists do what they can with ritualized elements such as titles, costuming, initiations, or vows of allegiance (all of which feature heavily in the Ku Klux Klan, for instance). The success of Islamic State at its peak illustrates the power of statelike structures, and its propaganda heavily emphasized the entitative qualities of its protostate in Iraq and Syria.[41]

The structure of an extremist ideology is designed to be filled with content providing a high level of entitativity, and extremist narratives tend to become more complex over time, drawing on an ever-wider variety of information sources. The more content is generated, the more entitativity accrues to the movement.

The crisis-solution construct also aims to address uncertainty. As discussed in chapter 4, extremist ideologies argue that the in-group has reached a watershed moment that requires dramatic, decisive action, which the ideology also clearly delineates.

The most common extremist crisis narratives—conspiratorial, dystopian, and apocalyptic—further address uncertainty. As noted in chapter 4, conspiracy theories are a powerful tool for "making sense" of the world. They contextualize problems that afflict an in-group by attributing them to deliberate, comprehensible actions by an out-group. Although the theories themselves are intricate, their conclusions are straightforward: the in-group's problems stem from the out-group's actions. Countering the out-group solves the problems.

Dystopian and apocalyptic crises are similarly clarifying and proactively explanatory.[42] They describe crises so sweeping and severe that extreme solutions are a foregone conclusion, cauterizing the need for deliberation. The nature of dystopian and apocalyptic crises minimizes demand for a strategy to "win the peace." In a dystopia, tearing down the corrupt system is a victory in itself. Because what replaces it cannot be worse, the details can be worked out at a later date.

For apocalyptic and millenarian adherents, the solution can be simpler still. Sometimes they only have to show up. Believers are mandated to take part in a cataclysmic event whose conclusion and aftermath are divinely ordained. The leaders of some apocalyptic groups may still make strategic choices, as Islamic State did in 2016 when it backed away from a prophesied battle it had previously promoted.[43] But at the level of most adherents, participation is the primary requirement.

Human beings are complex, and singular explanations for their actions are often elusive. There are several avenues for additional research to help clarify these questions. But after spending some years fruitlessly debating evidence-free views about the "root causes of violent extremism" with government officials and academics (the former more than the latter), I believe the uncertainty frame holds significant promise.

Uncertainty encompasses a number of social and political situations in which extremism rises up, including some scenarios that have led policymakers to embrace wrong explanations. Uncertainty also helps explain the actions of individuals who take up terrorism and extremism, particularly so-called lone wolves, who often experience traumatic disruptions to the status quo of their lives (such as the loss of a job or a parent) prior to taking part in violence. And there is extensive empirical experimental evidence that supports the uncertainty-identity premise, in addition to the complementary findings from my study of extremist texts.

Certainly, more work remains to be done, but uncertainty-identity theory and related research by social psychologists provide a more functional and better supported explanation of extremism and its causes than any of the current alternatives.

THE FUTURE OF EXTREMISM

Extremism has plagued humanity in cycles throughout recorded history. But if it has always been with us, so too have the forces that contain and defeat it. This battle will probably never end, but it is far from pointless. With each new wave, we rise again to the challenge and make gains for future generations.

Extremism is an old problem, but it is also always new. Extremist ideologies build on previous ideologies and evolve to fit the times. As human society becomes more complex and interconnected, so too does extremism. Extremism is a socially transmitted disease. Ideologies are transmitted when one person communicates with another. When communication technology changes, extremism changes as well.

The invention of the printing press is widely credited with starting a transformative change in Western society,

Extremism is an old problem, but it is also always new.

notably in spreading the ideas of the Protestant Reformation and associated apocalyptic beliefs.[1] The rise of electronic communication—radio, film, and television—was similarly transformative.

Broadcast and film provided powerful advantages to extremist movements with enough resources to exploit them, such as the Nazi regime.[2] But most extremist organizations are small and have limited resources. Professional film and video editing was once expensive and required highly technical skills. Broadcasting to more than a niche audience cost more still and was usually subject to government regulation.

These factors imposed a natural ceiling on what most extremist movements could achieve. If an extremist ideology cannot reach a mass audience, it cannot become a mass movement. Some movements managed to clear that hurdle, but in many cases, media limitations slowed their growth.

Social Media

When robust social media platforms came on the scene in the early twenty-first century, futurists waxed on about their transformative power. Some observers, including me, were skeptical, believing that changes in communications technology would be more incremental than revolutionary. We were wrong.[3]

Social media wrought dramatic changes in many different sectors of society in a very short period of time. For extremists, access to social media was a game changer. Extremists had been largely priced out of the broadcast revolution, but social media provided an inexpensive platform to reach massive audiences, emphasizing virality and controversy over social norms.

Extremists quickly established small and sometimes significant beachheads on social media, but Islamic State was the first to realize the potential of the new technology. Before the social media platforms developed a coherent response, Islamic State recruiters garnered thousands of supporters online, guided them in synchronized action, and produced highly professional propaganda using newly inexpensive video editing and publishing technologies. The organization's widely distributed content mixed ultraviolence with millenarian utopian visions in novel ways. The result was an unprecedented wave of jihadist extremist recruitment.[4]

While Islamic State's extreme violence dominated headlines, white nationalists were concurrently adopting and developing many of the same social media techniques and building an audience more gradually. These efforts started prior to the rise of Islamic State and blossomed in the late 2010s, fueling the current resurgence in ideological racism.[5]

There is evidence that social media use fosters increased tolerance and diversity in many users,[6] but the current generation of social media platforms provides benefits that uniquely empowered extremist movements relative to their mainstream counterparts.[7] While research on this subject is ongoing and the online environment is in constant flux, the current evidence suggests that social media leads a majority of people toward centrism and inclusivity but empowers and accelerates polarization and extremism for a significant minority. Factors aiding the spread of extremist views include the following:

• **Anonymity:** Extremist adherents can share their views and recruit with only a limited risk that their real identities will be exposed, insulating them from both legal and social repercussions.

• **Discovery:** Extremist recruiting is a game of small percentages. Most extremist movements appeal to small populations, and for violent extremists, the pool is even smaller. Extremists use social media searches, social network analysis, and algorithmically generated recommendations to find these small pools of people efficiently and to empower curious people to make contact with extremist adherents and recruiters with relative ease.

• **Physical security:** Before social media, the best way for a curious person to learn about a violent extremist movement was to meet one of its adherents in person. This was inherently risky because it involved spending time with potentially violent people. Today, the curious can interact with violent extremists in the digital world without any physical risk, building trust and comfort before meeting in the real world.

Uncertainty

Social psychology research strongly suggests that feelings of uncertainty make people more susceptible to extremism and empower the specific elements of extremism discussed in this book, such as in-group identification, out-group hostility, and crisis-solution narratives (such as conspiracy theories).

It is not surprising, therefore, that extremist movements are enjoying a wave of successes around the globe and that policymakers have identified violent extremism as one of the critical challenges of our time. Like extremism, uncertainty is with us always, but it may be particularly pronounced in today's world, for a number of reasons:

• **Speed of information:** With each new advancement in communications technology, more and more people have real-time, always-on access to information about global instability. It's not that global instability didn't exist before, but it wasn't necessarily a narrative drumbeat in ordinary lives. Today, information about global instability is continuously projected into people's homes and to devices they carry with them everywhere, which may increase feelings of uncertainty for some.

• **Amount of information:** Similarly, information is now far more available to ordinary people through the Internet and 24/7 media, but overwhelming information flows can lead to uncertainty (as seen in debates over everything from vaccination to climate change). When information sources proliferate, they must compete for public trust, making it difficult for ordinary people to evaluate the credibility of the information they receive and heightening uncertainty. At the same time, the vast stores of information available online provide fodder for extremist identity construction and for conspiracy theorists obsessed, as Hofstadter notes, with the accumulation of "evidence."

• **Quality of information:** Disinformation and misinformation are hardly new, but in the twenty-first century, they have been monetized, industrialized, and weaponized. "Fake news," conspiracy theories, and other forms of bad information are now profit vehicles for some and tools of state-sponsored influence for others. In addition to the power that bad information has to shape extremist narratives, the profusion of bad information makes some people uncertain about whether they can trust anyone to tell them the truth about the world.

• **Technological transformation:** In addition to the destabilizing influence of communication technology, other technological changes have placed many people in a state of economic flux as old industries collapse and are replaced by new ones that require specialized training or knowledge. As previously noted, unemployment and economic problems do not necessarily correlate to extremism, but sudden and bewildering changes in these arenas may. Other technologies—such as nuclear weapons—mean that instability in one part of the world can create fear and uncertainty everywhere.

• **Global migration and demographic change:** Over the last century, social and practical barriers to relocation and intermarriage among identity groups have crumbled in the face of cheap, rapid transportation and shifting legal and civil rights structures. Instability in several hotspots has also produced historically large refugee flows. All of these factors are reshaping religious and racial demographics around the world, which can trigger identity-based uncertainty—as evidenced by the prominence of refugees and immigration as themes in modern right-wing movements.

• **Superempowered superminorities:** All of these factors—social media, technological changes, cheap travel —are part of an environment in which relatively small groups of people can have an outsized impact on global politics. Islamic State, which has disrupted world politics and led to hundreds of thousands of deaths, represents a miniscule fraction of the world's population. Even measured against its eligible in-group, Sunni Muslims, active Islamic State supporters are less than a fraction of 1 percent of the available population of recruits. Through tactics such as terrorism, superempowered superminorities trigger substantial social and political uncertainty, which they then offer to resolve through ideology. Terrorism fuels extremism among the perpetrator's eligible in-group as well in as counterpart out-group movements. For instance, jihadists and right-wing extremists can feed each other's narratives in a symbiotic manner.[8]

Short of a civilizational collapse, all of these problems are likely here for the duration. Eventually, society will develop counterweights to their destabilizing influence, but that will take time, and the process of adaptation has barely begun. Because of all these factors, we are probably facing at least decades of increased extremist activity and associated violence.

Countering Extremism

Despite these challenges, we can hope to do better than simply endure. September 11, 2001, brought the challenge of extremism to the forefront of global politics, shaping a new era of conflict and setting new priorities for countries around the world. Politicians began an endless series of pledges to "defeat the ideology" that fuels terrorism, words that are now solemnly repeated after every terrorist attack.

Under intense political pressure to find solutions but reluctant to expand already prodigious military campaigns, policymakers adopted the age-old strategy of throwing everything at the wall to see what sticks, except that they rarely noted what stuck. Diplomats pushed pet projects such as development aid and education programs, even though the evidence strongly suggested they would not be effective.[9] A multitude of messaging campaigns were launched but with few visible successes and some fairly spectacular failures.[10]

Although some promising programs have managed to carve out a place at the table, they compete with many inferior programs, and policymakers have few objective measures to help them distinguish good from bad. Many factors contribute to the stagnation and inefficacy of the field known as Countering Violent Extremism (CVE) or Preventing Violent Extremism (PVE).[11] Among the most important problems are a lack of definitions for key terms, a lack of consensus models for extremism and radicalization, and a lack of interest in understanding extremism as a cross-ideological phenomenon.

These are not simply academic quibbles. Hundreds of millions of dollars have been spent on initiatives to defeat extremist ideologies and prevent radicalization by policymakers who cannot define extremism, ideology, or radicalization. This is a recipe for failure and a massive waste of resources. If we cannot define extremism or radicalization, we cannot define what success looks like. It is highly unlikely that the definitions and frameworks discussed in this book will be the final word in this debate, but they are designed to address some of the major deficiencies in the field and inspire further research on concrete questions—by defining the problem, understanding legitimacy, modeling radicalization, and understanding uncertainty.

Defining the Problem

As is discussed in chapter 2, extremism is currently defined in a variety of ways by policymakers and academics. Most of these definitions are problematic in one way or another, especially for designing programs that can be meaningfully evaluated.

Extremism is defined in this book as the belief that an in-group's success or survival can never be separated from the need for hostile action against an out-group. This definition offers several practical benefits for those seeking to counter extremism.

Perhaps foremost, this definition is not constrained to any one type of ideology. Although CVE efforts to date have focused overwhelmingly on jihadism, there is a growing recognition in the field that similar initiatives are needed for other types of extremism, whether white nationalists in Virginia, Hutu *génocidaires* in Rwanda, or ultranationalist Buddhists in Myanmar.

This definition also focuses on the core of the problem. Some supposed experts argue that countering jihadist extremism requires engagement with a wide range of Islamic religious teachings.[12] But efforts that do not focus clearly on mitigating a movement's hostile activity against an out-group are not countering extremism.

Definitional challenges also apply to the term *ideology*, which is used so vaguely that it takes on almost mystical qualities as a harbinger and proximate cause of bad ideas and bad behavior. By anchoring extremist ideology in the texts that encourage hostile action against out-groups, this book seeks to demystify the concept and encourage more specific countermessaging strategies.

Radicalized individuals do not necessarily engage with an extremist ideology in a sophisticated manner. Although extremist ideologies are often complex in their arguments, adherents pick and choose the elements that are meaningful to them. For some, this may entail little beyond a need to act violently against an out-group.[13]

Some adherents will steep themselves in an ideology. Others are satisfied knowing than some ideology— some internally coherent explanation for the shape of the world—exists. For many extremists, the charisma of the messenger or the ratification of existing violent impulses matters more than the ideology itself.

Yet ideology is ultimately the anchor for all of these dynamics, even when understood only by reference. The exact contents of an extremist propaganda message (or a mainstream counternarrative) may matter less than simply knowing that supporting arguments are always within reach.

Understanding Legitimacy

Since September 11, a core message from Western governments has been that groups like al Qaeda and ISIS are not legitimate in a religious sense.[14] President George W. Bush famously said that al Qaeda had "perverted" Islam. President Barack Obama's administration insisted on using the acronym ISIL or even the Arabic acronym Daesh because officials felt that referring to Islamic State by its chosen name would legitimize its connection to Islam. President Obama spoke more directly to the issue in 2016:

> Groups like ISIL are desperate for legitimacy. They try to portray themselves as religious leaders and holy warriors who speak for Islam. I refuse to give them legitimacy. We must never give them that legitimacy.[15]

Some elements of this rhetoric were positive. For one thing, both administrations were speaking not just (or even primarily) to Muslims but also to non-Muslim Americans who were confused about the reason for terrorist activity. Refuting the link between terrorist groups and the normative practices of Muslims is both important and admirable for wide audiences.

However, these attitudes leaked over into Countering Violent Extremism (CVE) initiatives, an entirely different arena. In dozens of policies and papers, government officials and nongovernmental activists discuss the goal of using religious figures, former extremists, and other tactics to delegitimize violent extremism.[16]

This approach is understandable, but the framework discussed in this book suggests that attacks on the legitimacy of extremist groups are likely to fail because legitimacy is the most central component of an extremist in-group's identity construction—the most highly developed and best-protected asset that any extremist group possesses. Legitimacy can be understood within this book's definition of extremism as the health, success and survival of the in-group. Hostile actions are taken against out-groups in order to ensure the health and legitimacy of the in-group, so direct attacks on extremist legitimacy may reinforce the notion that extreme measures are required to protect it.

Even worse, attacks on extremist legitimacy can provoke ideologues to craft counterarguments that lead the movement to radicalize even further. As British Israelism radicalized, it did so in the face of attacks from members of the eligible in-group—traditional Christians who cast aspersions on the developing ideology. Time and again, British Israelist authors responded to these criticisms by developing even more elaborate arguments in defense of its beliefs. These new justifications then formed the basis of additional theories that fueled more extreme beliefs.[17]

Similar dynamics are found in jihadist movements, where competition with mainstream Muslim scholars has hardened and expanded the complexity of extremist arguments. The escalation of radicalization from al Qaeda to the Islamic State was informed, in part, by internal and external criticisms of previous jihadist strategies and tactics.[18]

Although direct attacks on legitimacy may be unwise, *feeding* an extremist group's sense of legitimacy and entitlement is also an obvious and grave error. Western politicians who seek to conflate normative Muslim practices with those of Islamic State, for instance, are sending a clear message that they believe Islamic State does in fact represent some form of legitimate Muslim identity. Such rhetoric poses a genuine challenge to the legitimacy of

the nonextremist in-group and may make extremist arguments seem more compelling to more people.

Similar problems pertain to conflating systemic racism
or racial inequality with fully developed neo-Nazi ideologies. These are related but separate problems, and conflating them may have unintended consequences. Given that
extremist groups will generally absorb any information
source that supports their claims, messaging that awards
them any form of legitimacy is extremely dangerous and
counterproductive.

Modeling Radicalization

Beyond the question of definitions lies a question of processes. Here, again, consensus is sorely lacking. There are
many competing models, often using different nomencla-
ture. Some are too specific and are tailored to only one type
of extremism—while others are too vague to have practical application. Some scholars dispute that radicalization
even exists as a discrete, identifiable phenomenon.[19]

Nevertheless, people do adopt extremist views, and we
need a way to talk about that process if we want to do anything
about it. The models in chapter 5 are an attempt to describe
this process based on observations of extremist activity, with
an eye toward identifying opportunities to intervene.

The model of group radicalization offers additional
opportunities for narrative countermessaging that un-
dercuts ideological premises. The most vulnerable points

in this process are the extremist arguments connected to crisis—the linkage of an out-group's intrinsic identity to a crisis afflicting the in-group, the link between the extremist in-group and a solution for the crisis, and the very existence of a crisis in the first place. There is value in degrading other conceptual linkages promoted by extremist ideologies, but the framing of a crisis is most critical in mobilizing people toward violence and least likely to challenge the legitimacy of the eligible in-group.

The individual radicalization model also offers a number of possible intervention opportunities. While individual radicalization starts with some conditional acceptance of negative out-group characterizations and the crisis framing, the most critical stage in the process is the consideration of an extremist ideology. This is crucial both to the advancement of an extremist mindset, and, perhaps more important, it is the stage at which an individual is most likely to make social contact with extremist adherents and recruiters. Interventions that are pitched earlier in the radicalization process risk backfiring and pushing at-risk people into further engagement with extremism, while interventions later in the process face a much steeper challenge in dislodging ideas that have already taken hold.

Understanding Uncertainty

As previously noted, politicians and policymakers often gravitate toward programs that address the so-called root causes of terrorism. These typically focus on discredited explanations for extremism, such as poverty, lack of education, and undemocratic governance.

Although these structural factors are not proximate causes of extremism, there is good reason to believe that dramatic uncertainty-producing changes in these social and political tent poles may be linked to increased extremism. The experimental evidence for this premise is strong. Additional research should examine how this potentially works in the real world by studying the emergence of significant extremist movements in historical context.

With more study, it may be possible to craft pragmatic policies to prevent extremism by monitoring and potentially intervening in situations that are likely to create significant amounts of uncertainty in a specific region. For instance, if a local economy suddenly collapses (or surges), it may be useful to keep tabs on how that change is being processed and examine whether steps can be taken to reduce uncertainty.

Similarly, the uncertainty framing argues against certain strategies that have been attempted since September 11, such as instigating regime change in a country that is currently stable, even if that country suffers from oppression or other problems. Islamic State was the primary beneficiary of just such a strategy in Iraq, and it exploited the uncertainty caused by the initial invasion and the mismanagement of the aftermath.[20]

Obviously, extremism is not the only problem in the world, and many different pragmatic and idealistic considerations must be weighed when making policy decisions. There are other moral dimensions to making decisions based solely on the extremism/uncertainty frame. People suffering from poverty or injustice in relatively stable conditions may suffer as much as or more than those in uncertain conditions. But well-intentioned policies designed to aid people who are suffering should not be conflated with policies to combat extremism. These are separate pursuits and should be pursued separately.

Conclusion

The persistence of extremism in human history can be discouraging. It is difficult to accept that we are doomed to repeat such costly cycles of destruction. Yet humanity progresses despite it all. Steven Pinker argues in his book *The Better Angels of Our Nature: Why Violence Has Declined*, that there is reason to think that violence has declined throughout history as a proportion of all human activity, and that measures of health, happiness, and prosperity have improved.[21] Although some take issue with Pinker's argument in its entirety, many people (perhaps most) see an arc of progress stretching throughout history—painfully slow at times, and our two steps forward are too often followed by one back. But progress nonetheless.

Arguably, it is the very tension between extremism and inclusivity that produces social progress. Institutionalized slavery in the United States ended after just such a contest.[22]

Humanity may march forward over that long arc, but we cannot take progress for granted. During the Inquisitions, the conquest of the Americas, the African slave trade, World War II, and the prolonged conflicts in Iraq and Syria, ascendant extremism has again and again resulted in unbearable atrocities.

Extremists constantly evolve to meet the times, whether by adopting new technologies to spread their ideologies or by redefining in-group and out-group identities. Our efforts to counter extremism must also evolve.

The relative pace of institutional change creates a virtually unavoidable gap between the rise of an extremist movement and a successful response. Mainstream institutions reduce uncertainty—and thus extremism—primarily by providing stability, but the tradeoff can produce inertia when change is necessary.

Nevertheless, we can do better. The new communications technologies that empower extremists can also be used to detect their arrival and diagnose their importance. Both the rise of Islamic State and the resurgence of white nationalism were clearly visible online before most

Arguably, it is the very the tension between extremism and inclusivity that produces social progress. Institutionalized slavery in the United States ended after just such a contest.

analysts acknowledged their changing threat.[23] Our improved understanding of online social networks can provide a critical early warning about the growth of extremist movements and escalating radicalization.

Finally, we can begin to approach the problem of extremism as a field worthy of study in its own right and worthy of study across ideological boundaries. After September 11, those who sought to study terrorism were faced with a poorly defined field of study that encompassed many complex, multidisciplinary problems. In the ensuing years, the once shaky arena of terrorism studies has gradually solidified, thanks to a profusion of research by skilled professionals.[24]

Extremism is the field behind the field of terrorism, and it merits increased focus and prominence as a discrete academic subject. It may fall most securely within the discipline of social psychology, but extremism also requires a multidisciplinary approach encompassing history, politics, economics, religion, individual psychology, and more. Perhaps most important, extremism studies must include approaches that incorporate the comparative study of multiple ideologies. While it makes sense to focus on ascendant and escalating movements, cross-ideological study empowers insights that are obscured when viewing the problem through a single lens. When we study diverse extremist movements, we can identify what important principles they have in common and strip away superficialities.

Deep dives into specific ideologies such as jihadism and white nationalism remain vitally important, but we must also acknowledge the category-defying nature of extremism belief in order to combat it most effectively and to respond quickly to the rise of new and unexpected movements. We must understand extremism as it exists in the real world—an enduring part of human society that transcends demographics.

apocalyptic belief
The belief that out-groups will precipitate a comprehensive end to history in the not-too-distant future.

apostasy
The belief that substantially wrong beliefs or practices can disqualify an otherwise eligible person from membership in an in-group. Extremists often use this term interchangeably with **heresy**.

beliefs
The shared creed of a group, most importantly its values, but including secondary elements such as cosmology or metaphysics.

categorization
The act of understanding yourself to be a member of an in-group and determining whether others are part of your in-group or an out-group.

conspiracy belief
The belief that out-groups are engaged in secret actions to control in-group outcomes.

crisis
A pivotal event that requires an active response from the in-group.

crisis-solution construct
The claim that an in-group crisis has been caused by an out-group, and that the in-group can solve the crisis through hostile action against the out-group.

discrimination
Nonviolent hostile actions against an out-group, often in the form of denying out-group members benefits that are available to in-group members.

* *Note:* Terms are defined here within the context of extremism. Most of these terms have other meanings in ordinary contexts.

dystopian belief
The belief that out-groups have successfully oriented society to disadvantage the in-group.

eligible in-group
The broad identity collective that an extremist organization claims to represent and from which it seeks to recruit.

existential threat
The belief that out-groups threaten the survival of the in-group

extremism
The belief that an in-group's success or survival can never be separated from the need for hostile action against an out-group.

extremist ideology
A collection of texts, usually in narrative form, that describe who is part of an in-group and who is part of an out-group, and how an in-group should interact with out-groups.

extremist in-group
An identity collective consisting of an extremist movement or organization, usually including both formal members and active supporters.

genocide
Systematic slaughter of out-group members on a large scale.

harassment
Intentionally making out-groups unwelcome in the presence of the in-group.

hate crime
Non-systematic violence against out-group members.

heresy
The belief that substantially wrong beliefs or practices can disqualify an otherwise eligible person from membership in an in-group. Extremists often use this term interchangeably with **apostasy**.

identity
The set of qualities that are understood to make a person or group distinct from other persons or groups.

identity collective
A group of people who are defined by a common nation, religion, race, or some other shared trait, interest or concern.

impurity
Corruption of in-group beliefs, practices or traits, sometimes including the infiltration of out-group beliefs, practices and traits.

ineligible in-group
In-group members who are at risk of being expelled from the in-group, in the view of an extremist movement.

in-group
The group to which one belongs; organized around a shared identity, such as religion, race, or nationality.

legitimacy
The belief that an identity collective has a right to exist and may be rightfully defined, maintained, and protected.

millenarian belief
The belief that an event is fast approaching that will lead to end of the current world and the establishment of a utopian world.

oppression
Aggressive and systematic discrimination against an out-group, sometimes including systematic violence, usually involving an explicit legal framework

out-group
A group of people who are excluded from a specific in-group.

practices
What members of an identity group do and how they are expected to behave.

purity
The measure of how closely an in-group conforms to the prototypical in-group identity described by an ideology.

radicalization into extremism
The escalation of an in-group's extremist orientation in the form of increasingly negative views about an out-group or the endorsement of increasingly hostile or violent actions against an out-group.

segregation
The physical separation of an in-group from out-groups.

social identification
An act of self-categorization in which an individual understands one's self to be part of an in-group.

solution
Specific hostile actions that extremists argue in-groups should take against out-groups to resolve a crisis.

terrorism
Public violence targeting noncombatants, carried out by nongovernmental individuals or groups, in order to advance a political or ideological goal or amplify a political or ideological message.

traits
Descriptive qualities that apply to group members, including physical (such as skin tone or hair type), mental (intelligence or creativity), social (dialect, slang, and accents), or spiritual (virtuousness or piety).

triumphalism
The belief that the in-group successes can only be maintained by escalating hostile acts targeting out-groups.

violent extremism
The belief that an in-group's success or survival can never be separated from the need for violence against an out-group.

Chapter 1: Delenda Est

1. Jacobellis v. Ohio, 378 U.S. 184, 197 (1964) (Stewart, J., concurring).

2. "Extremism," accessed March 15, 2018, from Merriam-Webster.com. https://www.merriam-webster.com/dictionary/extremism.

3. D. Elaine Pressman, "Risk Assessment Decisions for Violent Political Extremism," report 2009–02, Public Safety Canada, Government of Canada, 2007, October 2009.

4. J. C. Van Es and Daniel J. Koenig, "Social Participation, Social Status and Extremist Political Attitudes," *Sociological Quarterly* 17, no. 1 (1976): 16–26; Lasse Lindekilde, "Neo-liberal Governing of 'Radicals': Danish Radicalization Prevention Policies and Potential Iatrogenic Effects," *International Journal of Conflict and Violence* 6, no. 1 (2012): 109; Cas Mudde, "Right-Wing Extremism Analyzed," *European Journal of Political Research* 27, no. 2 (1995): 203–224.

5. Charles S. Liebman, "Extremism as a Religious Norm," *Journal for the Scientific Study of Religion* (1983): 75–86.

6. Lorraine Bowman-Grieve, "Anti-abortion Extremism Online," *First Monday* 14, no. 11 (2009); Polina Zeti and Elena Zhirukhina, "Information Opposition to Extremism as a Way to Reduce Tension in the Northern Caucasus," *Caucasus & Globalization* 6, no. 2 (2012): 22–30.

7. Albert Breton, Gianluigi Galeotti, Pierre Salmon, and Ronald Wintrobe, eds., *Political Extremism and Rationality* (New York: Cambridge University Press, 2002), 25; Charlie Edwards and Luke Gribbon, "Pathways to Violent Extremism in the Digital Era," *RUSI Journal* 158, no. 5 (2013): 40–47; Arie W. Kruglanski, Katarzyna Jasko, Marina Chernikova, Michelle Dugas, and David Webber, "To the Fringe and Back: Violent Extremism and the Psychology of Deviance," *American Psychologist* 72, no. 3 (2017): 217.

8. Google Scholar search, accessed September 10, 2017. A search for *jihadism* yielded 10,600 results, compared to 3,370 for *white nationalism*.

9. Emily Shugerman, "Sebastian Gorka Said White Supremacists Were 'Not the Problem' Days before Charlottesville," *The Independent*, August 14, 2017; Nathan Guttman, "Sebastian Gorka's Wife Pushed Cuts to Group Fighting White Supremacists," *Forward*, August 16, 2017, http://forward.com/news/breaking-news/380075/sebastian-gorkas-wife-pushed-cuts-to-group-fighting-white-supremacists.

10. Ben Kiernan, "The First Genocide: Carthage, 146 BC," *Diogenes* 51, no. 3 (2004): 27–39.

11. Erich S. Gruen, "Romans and Others," *A Companion to the Roman Republic* (2006): 457–477.

12. Kiernan, "The First Genocide."

13. Norman M. Naimark, *Genocide: A World History* (New York: Oxford University Press, 2016), 5–12.

14. Shimon Applebaum, "The Zealots: The Case for Revaluation," *Journal of Roman Studies* 61 (1971): 155–170; H. Paul Kingdon, "Who Were the Zealots and Their Leaders in AD 66?," *New Testament Studies* 17, no. 1 (1970): 68–72.

15. David Goodblatt, "Priestly Ideologies of the Judean Resistance," *Jewish Studies Quarterly* 3, no. 3 (1996): 225–249; Sidney B. Hoenig, "The Sicarii in Masada: Glory or Infamy?," *Tradition: A Journal of Orthodox Jewish Thought* 11, no. 1 (1970): 5–30.

16. Josephus, *The Wars of the Jews*, book 1, chap. 13, ca. 78 CE, http://www.gutenberg.org/files/2850/2850-h/2850-h.htm; Hoenig, "The Sicarii in Masada."

17. For only the most recent challenge to the Sicarii narrative, see Ilan Ben Zion, "New Archaeology Shows 'Refugee Camp,' Not Just Rebels, Atop Masada," September 10, 2017, http://forward.com/news/israel/382132/exclusive-new-archaeology-shows-refugee-camp-not-just-rebels-atop-masada.

18. Cyril Glassé, *The New Encyclopedia of Islam*, 3rd ed. (Lanham, MD: Rowman & Littlefield, 2008), 255.

19. Everett K. Rowson, ed., *The History of al-Tabari*, vol. 22, *The Marwanid Restoration: The Caliphate of 'Abd al-Malik AD 693–701/AH 74–81* (Albany: State University of New York Press, 1989), 35n.

20. Elaine Pagels, "Irenaeus, the 'Canon of Truth,' and the 'Gospel of John,' 'Making a Difference' through Hermeneutics and Ritual," *Vigilae Christianae* 56, no. 4 (2002): 339–371.

21. Keith Lewinstein, "Making and Unmaking a Sect: The Heresiographers and the Ṣufriyya," *Studia Islamica* (1992): 75–96.

22. Nelly Lahoud, *The Jihadis' Path to Self-Destruction* (London: Hurst, 2010), 31–32.

23. Thomas Sizgorich, *Violence and Belief in Late Antiquity: Militant Devotion in Christianity and Islam* (Philadelphia: University of Pennsylvania Press, 2010), 17–18.

24. Josef W. Meri, ed., *Medieval Islamic Civilization: An Encyclopedia,* Vol. 1 (New York: Routledge, 2005), 436.

25. Daniel Walther, "A Survey of Recent Research on the Albigensian Cathari," *Church History* 34, no. 2 (1965): 146–177, http://www.jstor.org/stable/3162901; Catherine Léglu, Rebecca Rist, and Claire Taylor, eds., *The Cathars and the Albigensian Crusade: A Sourcebook* (New York: Routledge, 2013), 37–38.

26. Colin Tatz and Winton Higgins, *The Magnitude of Genocide* (Santa Barbara, CA: Praeger, 2016), 214; Naimark, *Genocide*, 2016, 31–33.

27. Naimark, *Genocide*, 34–38.

28. Juan Ginés de Sepúlveda, "Democrates Alter, or, on the Just Causes for War against the Indians," 1544, http://www.columbia.edu/acis/ets/CCREAD/sepulved.htm.

29. Naimark, *Genocide*, 48–49.

30. John Francis Maxwell, *Slavery and the Catholic Church: The History of Catholic Teaching Concerning the Moral Legitimacy of the Institution of Slavery* (London: Barry Rose Publishers in Association with the Anti-Slavery Society for the Protection of Human Rights, 1975), 45–91.

31. Drew Gilpin Faust, ed., *The Ideology of Slavery: Proslavery Thought in the Antebellum South, 1830–1860* (Baton Rouge: Louisiana State University Press, 1981).

32. Thomas R. Dew, *Review of the Debate [on the Abolition of Slavery] in the Virginia Legislature of 1831 and 1832* (Richmond, VA: T. W. White, 1832).

33. Faust, *The Ideology of Slavery*, 9–12.

34. Junius P. Rodriguez, ed., *Slavery in the United States: A Social, Political, and Historical Encyclopedia*, vol. 1 (Santa Barbara, CA: ABC-CLIO, 2007), 165, 497–498.

35. Richard J. Evans, *The Coming of the Third Reich* (New York: Penguin, 2005), Kindle locations 816–947.

36. Rudolph J. Rummel, *Democide: Nazi Genocide and Mass Murder* (New York: Transaction, 1992), 11–14.

37. Robert S. Wistrich, *Hitler's Apocalypse: Jews and the Nazi Legacy* (London: Weidenfeld & Nicolson, 1985), chaps. 9–12.

38. J. M. Berger, "Without Prejudice: What Sovereign Citizens Believe," Program on Extremism, George Washington University, June 2016, https://cchs.gwu.edu/sites/cchs.gwu.edu/files/downloads/Occasional%20Paper_Berger.pdf.

39. Naimark, *Genocide*, 86–90, 131–136.

40. J. M. Berger, *Jihad Joe: Americans Who Go to War in the Name of Islam* (Washington, DC: Potomac Books, 2011), Kindle locations 203–334.

41. Ibid., Kindle locations 1167–1198, 1165–1327; Vesna Pesic, "Serbian Nationalism and the Origins of the Yugoslav Crisis," 1996, https://www.usip.org/sites/default/files/pwks8.pdf; interview with Peter Galbraith, former

U.S. ambassador to Croatia, May 2009; interview with Tony Lake, former U.S. national security advisor, May 2009; interview with Fotini Christia, assistant professor of political science, Massachusetts Institute of Technology, May 2009.

42. "Bosnia & Herzegovina: Extremism & Counter-Extremism," Counter Extremism Project, 2017, https://www.counterextremism.com/countries/bosnia-herzegovina; Ron Synovitz, "Slobo Street? Serb Nationalists Redouble Efforts to Honor Milosevic," Radio Free Europe/Radio Liberty, August 12, 2017, https://www.rferl.org/a/serbia-milosevic-nationalists-street-name/28672918.html.

43. Lawrence Wright, *The Looming Tower: Al-Qaeda and the Road to 9/11* (New York: Knopf, 2006).

44. Jessica Stern and J. M. Berger, *ISIS: The State of Terror* (New York: HarperCollins, 2015), chaps. 5–6.

45. "Syrian President Bashar al-Assad: Facing Down Rebellion," BBC News, October 21, 2015, http://www.bbc.com/news/10338256.

46. Tom Miles, "Syrian Opposition 'Fed Up with Terrorists,' Seeks Help against Assad," Reuters, March 26, 2017, http://www.reuters.com/article/us-mideast-crisis-syria-opposition-idUSKBN16X0ZR.

47. Cole Bunzel, "Abandoning al-Qaida: Tahrir al-Sham and the Concerns of Sami al-'Uraydi," *Jihadica*, May 12, 2017, http://www.jihadica.com/abandoning-al-qaida.

48. Charles R. Lister, *The Syrian Jihad: Al-Qaeda, the Islamic State and the Evolution of an Insurgency* (New York: Oxford University Press, 2016), chap. 9.

49. Ian Fisher, "In Palestinian Power Struggle, Hamas Moderates Talk on Israel," *New York Times*, May 1, 2017, https://www.nytimes.com/2017/05/01/world/middleeast/hamas-fatah-palestinians-document.html.

50. "From Alt Right to Alt Lite: Naming the Hate," Anti-Defamation League, accessed September 15, 2017, https://www.adl.org/education/resources/backgrounders/from-alt-right-to-alt-lite-naming-the-hate.

51. Thomas Fuller, "Extremism Rises among Myanmar Buddhists," *New York Times*, June 20, 2013, http://www.nytimes.com/2013/06/21/world/asia/extremism-rises-among-myanmar-buddhists-wary-of-muslim-minority.html.

Chapter 2: What Is Extremism?

1. Hannah Arendt, "Ideology and Terror: A Novel Form of Government," *Review of Politics* 15, no. 3 (1953): 303–327.

2. Henri Tajfel, M. J. Billig, R. P. Bundy, and Claude Flament, "Social Categorization and Intergroup Behaviour," *European Journal of Social Psychology* 1, no.

2 (1971): 149–178; Henry Tajfel, "Social Identity and Intergroup Behaviour," *Information (International Social Science Council)* 13, no. 2 (1974): 65–93; Henri Tajfel and John C. Turner, "An Integrative Theory of Intergroup Conflict," *Social Psychology of Intergroup Relations* 33, no. 47 (1979): 74; Henri Tajfel, "The Social Identity Theory of Intergroup Behavior," *Introducing Social Psychology* (New York: Penguin Books, 1978): 401–466.

3. These definitions can be quite individualized and peculiar. For instance, "Ideology is defined as a dislocated form of consciousness whereby one class is able to acquire and use for its own benefit the appropriated surplus labour and product." Edris Salim El Hassan, "On Ideology: The Case of Religion in Northern Sudan," PhD dissertation, University of Connecticut, 1980.

4. Jean Anyon, "Ideology and United States History Textbooks," *Harvard Educational Review* 49, no. 3 (1979): 361–386; Peter Wiles, "Ideology, Methodology, and Neoclassical Economics," *Journal of Post Keynesian Economics* 2, no. 2 (1979): 155–180; Nels Johnson, "Palestinian Refugee Ideology: An Enquiry into Key Metaphors," *Journal of Anthropological Research* 34, no. 4 (1978): 524–539; Louis Althusser, *On Ideology* (London: Verso, 2008).

5. Sarah Kendzior, "How Do You Become 'White' in America?," *De Correspondent*, September 1, 2016, https://thecorrespondent.com/5185/how-do-you -become-white-in-america/1466577856645-8260d4a7.

6. "Nuremberg Laws," *Holocaust Encyclopedia*, United States Holocaust Memorial Museum, accessed September 17, 2017, https://www.ushmm.org/wlc/en/ article.php?ModuleId=10007902.

7. See Jason K. Duncan, *Citizens or Papists? The Politics of Anti-Catholicism in New York, 1685–1821* (New York: Fordham University Press, 2005).

8. J. M. Berger, "Without Prejudice: What Sovereign Citizens Believe," Program on Extremism, George Washington University, June 2016.

9. Benedict Anderson and Richard O'Gorman, *Under Three Flags: Anarchism and the Anti-colonial Imagination* (London: Verso, 2005), 75.

10. Alpa Shah, "'The Muck of the Past': Revolution, Social Transformation, and the Maoists in India," *Journal of the Royal Anthropological Institute* 20, no. 2 (2014): 337–356.

11. Rudolf Rocker, *Anarchism and Anarcho-syndicalism* (London: Freedom Press, 1973).

12. "Murder and Extremism in the United States in 2016," Anti-Defamation League Report, Anti-Defamation League, New York, 2017, https://www.adl .org/education/resources/reports/murder-and-extremism-in-the-united-states -in-2016.

13. Mariah Blake, "Mad Men: Inside the Men's Rights Movement—and the Army of Misogynists and Trolls It Spawned," *Mother Jones*, January–February 2015; Jonathon Merritt, "How Christians Turned against Gay Conversion Therapy," *The Atlantic*, April 15, 2015.

14. For more on this topic, see Mia Bloom, *Bombshell: Women and Terrorism* (Philadelphia: University of Pennsylvania Press, 2012).

15. Benjamin Politowski, "Terrorism in Great Britain: The Statistics," U.K. House of Commons Briefing Library, June 9, 2016; Susanne Rippl and Christian Seipel, "Gender Differences in Right-Wing Extremism: Intergroup Validity of a Second-Order Construct," *Social Psychology Quarterly* 62, no. 4 (1999): 381–393.

16. For example, David Duke, "Defense of White Women and the Vicious Jewish Attack on Trump as the 'Anti-Christ!,'" *David Duke Radio Show*, February 20, 2016; "Pregnant White Women," Stormfront (forum thread), January 16, 2016.

17. Jessica Stern and J. M. Berger, *ISIS: The State of Terror* (New York: HarperCollins, 2015), 89–91.

18. Ibid., 216.

19. J. M. Berger, *Jihad Joe: Americans Who Go to War in the Name of Islam* (Washington, DC: Potomac Books, 2011), Kindle locations 1246, 1689, 4013–4022; "37,000 White Women Raped by Blacks in 2005," *White News Now*, August 14, 2014; "The Islamic Rape Epidemic of White Women and Children," Stormfront (forum thread), September 4, 2014.

20. Cassandra Vinograd, "ISIS Hurls Gay Men off Buildings, Stones Them: Analysts," NBC News, August 26, 2015, https://www.nbcnews.com/storyline/isis-terror/isis-hurls-gay-men-buildings-stones-them-analysts-n305171.

21. "Persecution of Homosexuals in the Third Reich," *Holocaust Encyclopedia*, United States Holocaust Memorial Museum, accessed September 20, 2017, https://www.ushmm.org/wlc/en/article.php?ModuleId=10005261.

22. Federal Bureau of Investigation, "Texas Reserve Militia," FBI Letterhead Memorandum, December 21, 1990, obtained by the author through the Freedom of Information Act.

23. "The Safety Valve," *Instauration*, June 1995; "Back Talk," *Instauration*, June 1995.

24. Donna Minkowitz, "How the Alt-Right Is Using Sex and Camp to Attract Gay Men to Fascism," *Slate*, June 5, 2017, http://www.slate.com/blogs/outward/2017/06/05/how_alt_right_leaders_jack_donovan_and_james_o_meara_attract_gay_men_to.html.

25. These definitions are adapted and revised from J. M. Berger, "Extremist Construction of Identity: How Escalating Demands for Legitimacy Shape and Define In-Group and Out-Group Dynamics," *International Centre for Counter-Terrorism—The Hague* 8, no. 7 (2017).

26. Alex P. Schmid, "The Definition of Terrorism," *The Routledge Handbook of Terrorism Research*, ed. Alex P. Schmid, 30–157 (New York: Routledge Handbooks Online, 2011).

Chapter 3: In-Groups and Out-Groups

1. Henri Tajfel and John C. Turner, "The Social Identity Theory of Intergroup Behavior" (1979), in *Political Psychology: Key Readings*, ed. John T. Jost and James Sidanius (New York: Psychology Press, 2004), 276–293.

2. J. M. Berger, "Extremist Construction of Identity: How Escalating Demands for Legitimacy Shape and Define In-Group and Out-Group Dynamics," *International Centre for Counter-Terrorism—The Hague* 8, no. 7 (2017).

3. Margaret R. Somers and Gloria D. Gibson, "Reclaiming the Epistemological Other: Narrative and the Social Constitution of Identity," CRSO Working Paper 499, Center for Research on Social Organization, June 1993.

4. Jonathan Friedman, "Myth, History, and Political Identity," *Cultural Anthropology* 7, no. 2 (1992): 194–210.

5. James E. Landing, *Black Judaism: Story of an American Movement* (Durham, NC: Carolina Academic Press, 2002); Stuart Kirsch, "Lost Tribes: Indigenous People and the Social Imaginary," *Anthropological Quarterly* (1997): 58–67.

6. Berger, "Extremist Construction of Identity."

7. Ibid.

8. Ibid.

9. Ibid.; Michael J. Vlach, "Various Forms of Replacement Theology," *Master's Seminary Journal* 20, no. 1 (2011): 57–69.

10. Jennifer K. Bosson, Amber B. Johnson, Kate Niederhoffer, and William B. Swann Jr., "Interpersonal Chemistry through Negativity: Bonding by Sharing Negative Attitudes about Others," *Personal Relationships*13, no. 2 (2006): 135–150, http://uwf.edu/svodanov/AS/Bonding-Social-Identity.pdf.

11. Shiraz Maher, *Salafi-Jihadism: The History of an Idea* (London: Hurst, 2016), 36–39; Hassan Hassan, "The Sectarianism of the Islamic State: Ideological Roots and Political Context," Carnegie Endowment for International Peace, June 13, 2016.

12. Bart D. Ehrman, *Lost Christianities: The Battles for Scripture and the Faiths We Never Knew* (New York: Oxford University Press, 2005).

13. "Heresy," accessed on March 19, 2018, from New Advent, *The Catholic Encyclopedia*. http://www.newadvent.org/cathen/07256b.htm.

14. Elaine Pagels, "Irenaeus, the 'Canon of Truth,' and the 'Gospel of John': 'Making a Difference' through Hermeneutics and Ritual," *Vigiliae christianae* 56, no. 4 (2002): 339–371.

15. Alexander Roberts and James Donaldson, eds., *The Ante-Nicene Fathers*. Vol. 1: *The Apostolic Fathers—Justin Martyr–Irenaeus* (Grand Rapids, MI: William B. Eerdmans, 1956); accessed in Kindle edition prepared by Matjaž Črnivec, *Against Heresies and Fragments* (Annotated). (Kindle Locations 8041-8099, 2012); Pagels, "Irenaeus, the 'Canon of Truth.'"

16. Sidney Z. Ehler and John B. Morrall, eds., *Church and State through the Centuries: A Collection of Historic Documents with Commentaries* (New York: Biblo and Tannen, 1967), 7–9.

17. Rosemary Ruether, *Faith and Fratricide: The Theological Roots of Anti-Semitism* (Eugene, OR: Wipf and Stock, 1996), 128–129.

18. Robert L. Wilken, *John Chrysostom and the Jews: Rhetoric and Reality in the Late Fourth Century* (Eugene, OR: Wipf and Stock, 2004), 68.

19. Thomas Sizgorich, *Violence and Belief in Late Antiquity: Militant Devotion in Christianity and Islam* (Philadelphia: University of Pennsylvania Press, 2012), 35–40.

20. Jennifer Barry, "Diagnosing Heresy: Ps.-Martyrius's Funerary Speech for John Chrysostom," *Journal of Early Christian Studies* 24, no. 3 (2016): 395–418.

21. Sizgorich, *Violence and Belief*, 108–111, 127–143.

22. Anita M. Waters, "Conspiracy Theories as Ethnosociologies: Explanation and Intention in African American Political Culture," *Journal of Black Studies* 28, no. 1 (1997): 112–125.

23. Thomas F. Pettigrew and Linda R. Tropp, "A Meta-analytic Test of Intergroup Contact Theory," *Journal of Personality and Social Psychology* 90, no. 5 (2006): 751; Keith N. Hampton, Chul-joo Lee, and Eun Ja Her, "How New Media Affords Network Diversity: Direct and Mediated Access to Social Capital through Participation in Local Social Settings," *new media & society* 13, no. 7 (2011): 1031–1049; Eytan Bakshy, Solomon Messing, and Lada A. Adamic, "Exposure to Ideologically Diverse News and Opinion on Facebook," *Science* 348, no. 6239 (2015): 1130–1132.

24. "U.S. Muslims Concerned about Their Place in Society, but Continue to Believe in the American Dream," Pew Research Center, July 26, 2017, p. 128, http://assets.pewresearch.org/wp-content/uploads/sites/11/2017/07/25171611/U.S.-MUSLIMS-FULL-REPORT.pdf.

25. Ted Goertzel, "Belief in Conspiracy Theories," *Political Psychology* (1994): 731–742; Timothy Zaal, "I Used to Be a Neo-Nazi. Charlottesville Terrifies Me," *Politico*, August 18, 2017, http://www.politico.com/magazine/story/2017/08/18/former-neo-nazi-charlottesville-terrifies-me-215502.

Chapter 4: Crises and Solutions

1. H. J. Ingram, "A 'Linkage-Based' Approach to Combating Militant Islamist Propaganda: A Two-Tiered Framework for Practitioners," *International Centre for Counter-Terrorism—The Hague* 7, no. 6 (2016); H. J. Ingram, "The Strategic Logic of the 'Linkage-Based' Approach to Combating Militant Islamist Propaganda: Conceptual and Empirical Foundations," *International Centre for Counter-Terrorism—The Hague* 8, no. 6 (2017).

2. This is a subjective judgment. It should not be assumed that extremists understand the true history or nature of the eligible in-group that they claim to represent.

3. Aaron Zelin, "The Intellectual Origins of al-Qaeda's Ideology: The Abolishment of the Caliphate through the Afghan Jihad, 1924–1989," master's thesis, Brandeis University, 2010; Hassan Hassan, "The Sectarianism of the Islamic State: Ideological Roots and Political Context," Carnegie Endowment for International Peace, June 13, 2016.

4. Pedro Domingos, "The Role of Occam's Razor in Knowledge Discovery," *Data Mining and Knowledge Discovery* 3, no. 4 (1999): 409–425.

5. Allison G. Smith, "From Words to Action: Exploring the Relationship between a Group's Value References and Its Likelihood of Engaging in Terrorism," *Studies in Conflict & Terrorism* 27, no. 5 (2004): 409–437.

6. Hannah Darwin, Nick Neave, and Joni Holmes, "Belief in Conspiracy Theories: The Role of Paranormal Belief, Paranoid Ideation and Schizotypy," *Personality and Individual Differences* 50, no. 8 (2011): 1289–1293.

7. Hofstadter stipulates in his essay that he is using the word *paranoid* colloquially rather than clinically.

8. Richard Hofstadter, *The Paranoid Style in American Politics* (New York: Vintage, 2012), 36.

9. Ted Goertzel, "Belief in Conspiracy Theories," *Political Psychology* 15, no. 4 (1994): 731–742.

10. Anita M. Waters, "Conspiracy Theories as Ethnosociologies: Explanation and Intention in African American Political Culture," *Journal of Black Studies* 28, no. 1 (1997): 112–125.

11. Steve Oswald, "Conspiracy and Bias: Argumentative Features and Persuasiveness of Conspiracy Theories," Ontario Society for the Study of Argumentation, 2016.

12. Hofstadter, *The Paranoid Style*, 35.

13. J. M. Berger, "The *Turner* Legacy: The Storied Origins and Enduring Impact of White Nationalism's Deadly Bible," *International Centre for Counter-Terrorism—The Hague* 7, no. 8 (2016).

14. Berger, "The *Turner* Legacy."

15. Melissa Ames, "Engaging 'Apolitical' Adolescents: Analyzing the Popularity and Educational Potential of Dystopian Literature Post-9/11," *High School Journal* 97, no 1 (2013): 3–20; Alex Campbell, "Why Is Dystopian Fiction Still So Popular?," *The Guardian*, November 18, 2014, https://www.theguardian.com/childrens-books-site/2014/nov/18/hunger-games-dystopian-fiction-appeal-to-teenagers-alex-campbell.

16. J. M. Berger, "When? A Prophetical Novel of the Very Near Future," World Gone Wrong (blog), April 17. 2017, http://www.worldgonewrong.net/2017/04/when-prophetical-novel-of-very-near.html.

17. Patricia L. Dunmire, "Preempting the Future: Rhetoric and Ideology of the Future in Political Discourse," *Discourse & Society* 16, no. 4 (2005): 481–513; Keith Aoki and John Shuford, "Welcome to Amerizona—Immigrants Out! Assessing 'Dystopian Dreams' and 'Usable Futures' of Immigration Reform, and Considering Whether 'Immigration Regionalism' Is an Idea Whose Time Has Come," *Fordham Urban Law Journal* 38 (2010): 1.

18. Anwar al-Awlaki, "Lessons from the Companions Living as a Minority," paper presented at JIMAS Conference, University of Leicester, UK, August 2002.

19. Aric McBay, Lierre Keith, and Derrick Jensen, *Deep Green Resistance: Strategy to Save the Planet* (New York: Seven Stories Press, 2011).

20. Norman Cohn, *The Pursuit of the Millennium: Revolutionary Millenarians and Mystical Anarchists of the Middle Ages*, rev. ed. (New York: Oxford University Press, [1970] 2011), expanded Kindle edition locations 816–957.

21. "crisis," *Merriam-Webster*, https://www.merriam-webster.com/dictionary/crisis.

22. Jessica Stern and J. M. Berger, *ISIS: The State of Terror* (New York: HarperCollins, 2015), 104–125.

23. This section is adapted in part from J. M. Berger, "Extremist Construction of Identity: How Escalating Demands for Legitimacy Shape and Define In-Group and Out-Group Dynamics," *International Centre for Counter-Terrorism—The Hague* 8, no. 7 (2017).

24. "*Protocols of the Elders of Zion:* Timeline," *Holocaust Encyclopedia*, U.S. Holocaust Memorial Museum, https://www.ushmm.org/wlc/en/article.php?ModuleId=10007244; Sergei Nilus, *The Protocols and World Revolution: Including a Translation and Analysis of the "Protocols of the Meetings of the Zionist Men of Wisdom"* (Boston: Small, Maynard, 1920).

25. Richard Landes and Steven T. Katz, *The Paranoid Apocalypse: A Hundred-Year Retrospective on the Protocols of the Elders of Zion* (New York: NYU Press, 2012), 114.

26. Ibid. See also "*Protocols of the Elders of Zion:* Timeline."

27. Henry Ford, *The International Jew: Aspects of Jewish Power in the United States*, vol. 4. (Dearborn, MI: Dearborn Publishing Company, 1922).

28. H. Ben Judah, *When? A Prophetical Novel of the Very Near Future* (Vancouver: British Israel Association of Greater Vancouver, 1944).

29. Edward Rothstein, "The Anti-Semitic Hoax That Refuses to Die," *New York Times*, April 21, 2006; Emma Gray Ellis, "The Internet Protocols of the Elders of Zion," *Wired*, March 12, 2017.

30. Riaz Hassan, "Interrupting a History of Tolerance: Anti-Semitism and the Arabs," *Asian Journal of Social Science* 37, no. 3 (2009): 452–462; "Jordanian TV Series on 'Protocols of Elders of Zion': The Abhorred, Treacherous Jews Are the World's Masters, Corrupters, Executioners," Middle East Media Research Institute, April 2–16, 2017, https://www.memri.org/tv/jordan-media-director-protocols-elders-zion-abhorred-treacherous-jews.

31. Maura Conway, "Terrorism and the Making of the 'New Middle East': New Media Strategies of Hezbollah and al Qaeda," in *New Media and the New Middle East*, ed. Philip Seib (New York: Palgrave Macmillan, 2007), 235–258; Lawrence Wright, *The Terror Years: From al-Qaeda to the Islamic State* (New York: Vintage, 2017), 298.

32. Haroro J. Ingram, "Deciphering the Siren Call of Militant Islamist Propaganda: Meaning, Credibility, and Behavioural Change," The International Centre for Counter-Terrorism research paper, The Hague, September 2016.

33. Abdullahi A. An-Na'im, "Religious Minorities under Islamic Law and the Limits of Cultural Relativism," *Human Rights Quarterly* 9, no. 1 (1987): 1.

34. Dan Baum, "Legalize It All," *Harper's Magazine*, April 2016, https://harpers.org/archive/2016/04/legalize-it-all.

35. Janelle Jones, "The Racial Wealth Gap: How African-Americans Have Been Shortchanged out of the Materials to Build Wealth," Economic Policy Institute, February 13, 2017, http://www.epi.org/blog/the-racial-wealth-gap-how-african-americans-have-been-shortchanged-out-of-the-materials-to-build-wealth.

36. Kathy Marks, *Faces of Right Wing Extremism* (Wellesley, MA: Branden Books, 1996), 78, 134, 142.

37. James B. Jacobs and Kimberly Potter, *Hate Crimes: Criminal Law and Identity Politics* (New York: Oxford University Press, 2000).

38. Hannah Arendt, "Reflections on Violence," *Journal of International Affairs* 23, no. 1 (1969): 1–35; Martin Shubik, "Terrorism, Technology, and the Socioeconomics of Death," *Comparative Strategy* 16, no. 4 (1997): 399–414.

39. J. M. Berger, "A Definition of Terrorism," Intelwire.com, June 21, 2015, http://news.intelwire.com/2015/06/a-definition-of-terrorism.html.

40. Ellen Knickmeyer, "Blood on Our Hands," *Foreign Policy*, October 25, 2010; Bobby Ghosh, "An Eye for an Eye," *Time*, February 26, 2006.

41. Stern and Berger, *ISIS*, 281.

42. Karl Ove Knausgaard, "Inside the Warped Mind of Anders Breivik," *The Telegraph*, July 18, 2015, reprinted July 22, 2016, http://www.telegraph.co.uk/news/2016/07/22/anders-breivik-inside-the-warped-mind-of-a-mass-killer.

43. "The 'Final Solution': Background & Overview," Jewish Virtual Library, accessed September 23, 2017, http://www.jewishvirtuallibrary.org/background-and-overview-of-the-quot-final-solution-quot.

44. Berger, "The *Turner* Legacy."

45. Norman M. Naimark, *Genocide: A World History* (New York: Oxford University Press, 2016), 48–56; Walter Richmond, *The Circassian Genocide* (Rutgers, NJ: Rutgers University Press, 2013), 3–8.

46. "Documenting Numbers of Victims of the Holocaust and Nazi Persecution," *Holocaust Encyclopedia*, U.S. Holocaust Memorial Museum, accessed September 23, 2017, https://www.ushmm.org/wlc/en/article.php?ModuleId=10008193.

47. Sam Greenlee, *The Spook Who Sat by the Door: A Novel* (Detroit, MI: Wayne State University Press, 1990).

48. This section is adapted in part from Berger, "The *Turner* Legacy."

49. Lottie L. Joiner, "After Thirty Years, a Controversial Film Re-emerges," *The Crisis*, November/December 2003, 41.

50. Greenlee's suspicions are not easily dismissed as paranoia, given the activities of the FBI under its COINTELPRO (counterintelligence program) projects at the time. The claim is more fully explored in the documentary *Infiltrating Hollywood: The Spook Who Sat by the Door* (ChiTrini Productions, 2011).

51. J. M. Berger, "The John Franklin Letters," WorldGoneWrong.net, September 12, 2016, http://www.worldgonewrong.net/2016/09/the-john-franklin-letters.html.

Chapter 5: Radicalization

1. Portions of this section are adapted from J. M. Berger, "Making CVE Work: A Focused Approach Based on Process Disruption," *International Centre for Counter-Terrorism—The Hague* 7, no. 5 (2016).

2. Kevin B. Goldstein, "Unemployment, Inequality and Terrorism: Another Look at the Relationship between Economics and Terrorism," *Undergraduate Economic Review* 1, no. 1 (2005): 6, http://digitalcommons.iwu.edu/cgi/viewcontent.cgi?article=1006&context=uer; James A. Piazza, "The Determinants of Domestic Right-Wing Terrorism in the USA: Economic Grievance, Societal Change and Political Resentment," *Conflict Management and Peace Science* 34, no. 1 (2015): 52–80, http://journals.sagepub.com/doi/abs/10.1177/0738894215570429; James A. Piazza, "Rooted in Poverty?: Terrorism, Poor Economic Development, and Social Cleavages," *Terrorism and Political Violence* 18, no. 1 (2006): 159–177, http://www.tandfonline.com/doi/abs/10.1080/095465590944578; Edward Newman, "Exploring the 'Root Causes' of Terrorism," *Studies in Conflict and Terrorism* 29, no. 8 (2006): 749–772, http://www.tandfonline.com/doi/abs/10.1080/10576100600704069; Andreas E. Feldmann and Maiju Perälä, "Reassessing the Causes of Nongovernmental Terrorism in Latin America," *Latin American Politics and Society* 46, no. 2 (2004): 101–132, http://onlinelibrary.wiley.com/doi/10.1111/j.1548-2456.2004.tb00277.x/abstract.

3. Efraim Benmelech and Esteban F. Klor, *What Explains the Flow of Foreign Fighters to ISIS?*,. NBER Working Paper No. 22190, National Bureau of Economic Research, 2016, http://www.nber.org/papers/w22190.

4. Nate Rosenblatt, "All Jihad Is Local: What ISIS' Files Tell Us about Its Fighters," New America, Washington, DC, 2016.

5. Diego Gambetta and Steffen Hertog, "Uncivil Engineers: The Surprising Link between Education and Jihad," *Foreign Affairs*, March 10, 2016, https://www.foreignaffairs.com/articles/2016-03-10/uncivil-engineers.

6. C. Berrebi, "Evidence about the Link between Education, Poverty and Terrorism among Palestinians," *Peace Economics, Peace Science and Public Policy* 13, no. 1 (2007), http://www.degruyter.com/view/j/peps.2007.13.issue-1/peps.2007.13.1.1101/peps.2007.13.1.1101.xml.

7. Ibid.

8. Rik Coolsaet, "Facing the Fourth Foreign Fighters Wave: What Drives Europeans to Syria, and to Islamic State? Insights from the Belgian Case," Egmont Paper 81, Royal Institute for International Relations, Brussels, March 2016, http://aei.pitt.edu/73708.

9. Michael K. Jerryson and Mark Juergensmeyer, eds., *Buddhist Warfare* (New York: Oxford University Press, 2010), 92.

10. Ibid., 160–164; Francis Wade, *Myanmar's Enemy Within* (Chicago: University of Chicago Press, 2017).

11. Andrew Hough, "Norway Shooting: Anders Behring Breivik Plagiarised 'Unabomber,'" *The Telegraph*, July 24, 2011.

12. For example, Stephen Kinzer, "French, British Colonialism Grew a Root of Terrorism," *Boston Globe*, February 15, 2015; Richard J. Pech and Bret W. Slade, "Religious Fundamentalism and Terrorism: Why Do They Do It and What Do They Want?," *Foresight* 8, no. 1 (2006): 8–20.

13. J. M. Berger, "Extremist Construction of Identity: How Escalating Demands for Legitimacy Shape and Define In-Group and Out-Group Dynamics," *International Centre for Counter-Terrorism—The Hague*, 8, no. 7 (2017); J. M. Berger, "Deconstruction of Identity Concepts in Islamic State Propaganda: A Linkage-Based Approach to Counter-Terrorism Strategic Communications," paper presented at the First European Counter Terrorism Centre (ECTC) Conference on Online Terrorist Propaganda, Europol, The Hague, June 9, 2017; J. M. Berger, "Countering Islamic State Messaging through 'Linkage-Based' Analysis," *International Centre for Counter-Terrorism—The Hague* 8, no. 2 (2017).

14. J. M. Berger, "Tailored Online Interventions: The Islamic State's Recruitment Strategy," *CTC Sentinel* 8, no. 10 (October 2015); Berger, "Making CVE Work."

15. For more on this, see H. J. Ingram, *The Charismatic Leadership Phenomenon in Radical and Militant Islamism* (New York: Routledge, 2016).

16. William McCants, *The ISIS Apocalypse: The History, Strategy, and Doomsday Vision of the Islamic State* (New York: Macmillan, 2015), 34–41.

17. For a discussion of this, see Ron Rosenbaum, *Explaining Hitler: The Search for the Origins of His Evil* (Boston: Da Capo Press, [1998] 2014).

18. Aubrey Burl, *God's Heretics: The Albigensian Crusade* (Stroud, Gloucestershire, UK: History Press, 2005), chap. 6 et al.

19. Hannah Arendt, "Ideology and Terror: A Novel Form of Government," *Review of Politics* 15, no. 3 (1953): 303–327.

20. Berger, "Making CVE Work."

21. Clark McCauley and Sophia Moskalenko, "Mechanisms of Political Radicalization: Pathways toward Terrorism," *Terrorism and Political Violence* 20, no. 3 (2008): 415–433.

22. Stephen Kinzer, "French, British Colonialism Grew a Root of Terrorism," *Boston Globe*, February 11, 2015, https://www.bostonglobe.com/

opinion/2015/02/11/french-british-colonialism-bred-root-terrorism/GSaZ bcZuqXtbRE9CiwWPcO/story.html; "Oppression of Muslims Only Fosters Terrorism, Pakistani Leader Warns General Assembly," *UN News*, September 19, 2006, http://www.un.org/apps/news/story.asp?NewsID=19893.

23. James Silver, John Horgan, and Paul Gill, "Foreshadowing Targeted Violence: Assessing Leakage of Intent by Public Mass Murderers," *Aggression and Violent Behavior* (December 2017).

24. J. M. Berger, "PATCON: The FBI's Secret War against the 'Patriot' Movement, and How Infiltration Tactics Relate to Radicalizing Influences," New America, May 2012.

25. Peter Byrne, "Anatomy of Terror: What Makes Normal People Become Extremists?," *New Scientist*, August 16, 2017, https://www.newscientist.com/ article/mg23531390-700-anatomy-of-terror-what-makes-normal-people -become-extremists.

26. Silver, Horgan, and Gill, "Foreshadowing Targeted Violence."

27. A review of several studies with citations can be found in Henri Tajfel and Michael Billic, "Familiarity and Categorization in Intergroup Behavior," *Journal of Experimental Social Psychology* 10, no. 2 (1974): 159–170.

28. Jason T. Siegel, William D. Crano, Eusebio M. Alvaro, Andrew Lac, David Rast, and Vanessa Kettering, "Dying to Be Popular: A Purposive Explanation of Adolescent Willingness to Endure Harm," in *Extremism and the Psychology of Uncertainty*, ed. Michael A. Hogg and Danielle L. Blaylock, 115–130 (Malden, MA: Wiley-Blackwell, 2012), Kindle location 3703.

29. Michael Hogg, "Self-Uncertainty, Social Identity, and the Solace of Extremism," in *Extremism and the Psychology of Uncertainty*, ed. Michael A. Hogg and Danielle L. Blaylock, 19–35 (Malden, MA: Wiley-Blackwell, 2012).

30. J. Richard Eiser, Tom Stafford, and Russell H. Fazio, "Prejudiced Learning: A Connectionist Account," *British Journal of Psychology* 100, no. 2 (2009): 399–413.

31. John T. Jost and Roderick M. Kramer, "The System Justification Motive in Intergroup Relations," in *From Prejudice to Intergroup Emotions: Differentiated Reactions to Social Groups*, ed. Diane M. Mackie and Eliot R. Smith, 227–246 (New York: Psychology Press, 2002).

32. Michèlle Bal and Kees van den Bos, "From System Acceptance to Embracing Alternative Systems and System Rejection: Tipping Points in Processes of Radicalization," *Translational Issues in Psychological Science* 3, no. 3 (2017): 241.

33. Ibid.

34. Emily Corner and Paul Gill, "A False Dichotomy? Mental Illness and Lone-Actor Terrorism," *Law and Human Behavior* 39, no 1 (2015): 23; Katherine M.

Ramsland, *Inside the Minds of Mass Murderers: Why They Kill* (Westport, CT: Praeger, 2005), 42.

35. John Lofland and Rodney Stark, "Becoming a World-Saver: A Theory of Conversion to a Deviant Perspective," *American Sociological Review* 30, no. 6 (1965): 862–875; Jessica Stern and J. M. Berger, *ISIS: The State of Terror* (New York: HarperCollins, 2015), 81; Richard Barrett, "Foreign Fighters in Syria," Soufan Group, June 2014, http://soufangroup.com/wp-content/uploads/2014/06/TSG-Foreign-Fighters-in-Syria.pdf; David C. Rapoport, ed., *Terrorism: The Fourth or Religious Wave* (Taylor & Francis, 2006), 345.

36. Bal and van den Bos, "From System Acceptance to Embracing Alternative Systems and System Rejection."

37. Hogg, "Self-Uncertainty, Social Identity, and the Solace of Extremism," Kindle location 1187.

38. Bal and van den Bos, "From System Acceptance to Embracing Alternative Systems and System Rejection."

39. Hogg, "Self-Uncertainty, Social Identity, and the Solace of Extremism," Kindle location 1279.

40. J. M. Berger, "The Metronome of Apocalyptic Time: Social Media as Carrier Wave for Millenarian Contagion," *Perspectives on Terrorism* 9, no. 4 (2015).

41. Amarnath Amarasingam and J. M. Berger, "With the Destruction of the Caliphate, the Islamic State Has Lost Far More Than Territory," *Monkey Cage* (blog), *Washington Post*, October 31, 2017, https://www.washingtonpost.com/news/monkey-cage/wp/2017/10/31/the-caliphate-that-was.

42. Alison McQueen, "The Apocalypse in U.S. Political Thought," *Foreign Affairs*, July 18, 2016, https://www.foreignaffairs.com/articles/united-states/2016-07-18/apocalypse-us-political-thought.

43. Adam Withnall, "Isis Loses 'Prophesied' Town of Dabiq to Syrian Rebels after Short Battle," *The Independent*, October 16, 2016, http://www.independent.co.uk/news/world/middle-east/isis-dabiq-loses-apocalyptic-prophesy-town-of-dabiq-to-syria-rebels-short-battle-a7363931.html.

Chapter 6: The Future of Extremism

1. Carolyn Jensen, "Review of the Printing Revolution in Early Modern Europe," *LORE: Rhetoric, Writing, Culture* 12 (2001); Colin Woodard, "The Power of Luther's Printing Press," *Washington Post*, December 18, 2015, https://www.washingtonpost.com/opinions/the-power-of-luthers-printing-press/2015/12/18/a74da424-743c-11e5-8d93-0af317ed58c9_story.html; Mark Edwards Jr., "Apocalypticism Explained: Martin Luther," Frontline,

accessed November 10, 2017, http://www.pbs.org/wgbh/pages/frontline/shows/apocalypse/explanation/martinluther.html.

2. Maja Adena, Ruben Enikolopov, Maria Petrova, Veronica Santarosa, and Ekaterina Zhuravskaya, "Radio and the Rise of the Nazis in Prewar Germany," *Quarterly Journal of Economics* 130, no. 4 (2015): 1885–1939.

3. J. M. Berger, "Internet Provides Terrorists with Tools—Just Like Everyone Else," Intelwire, July 31, 2011, http://news.intelwire.com/2011/07/internet-provides-terrorists-with-tools.html.

4. J. M. Berger, "#Unfollow: The Case for Kicking Terrorists off Twitter," *Foreign Policy*, February 20, 2013, http://foreignpolicy.com/2013/02/20/unfollow; Jessica Stern and J. M.Berger, *ISIS: The State of Terror* (New York: HarperCollins, 2015), chaps. 10–11.

5. J. M. Berger and Bill Strathearn, "Who Matters Online: Measuring Influence, Evaluating Content and Countering Violent Extremism in Online Social Networks," International Centre for the Study of Radicalisation and Politcal Terrorism, London, March 2013; J. M. Berger, "Nazis vs. ISIS on Twitter: A Comparative Study of White Nationalist and ISIS Online Social Media Networks," Program on Extremism, George Washington University, September 2016.

6. Pablo Barberá, "How Social Media Reduces Mass Political Polarization: Evidence from Germany, Spain, and the US," Working Paper, New York University, 2014; Levi Boxell, Matthew Gentzkow, and Jesse M. Shapiro, "Is the Internet Causing Political Polarization? Evidence from Demographics," NBER Working Paper No. 23258, National Bureau of Economic Research, 2017.

7. J. M. Berger, "The Toxic Mix of Extremism and Social Media," Nova Next, September 7, 2016, http://www.pbs.org/wgbh/nova/next/military/extremism-social-media.

8. Matenia Sirseloudi, "Dyadic Radicalisation via Internet Propaganda," paper presented at the Europol Conference on Online Terrorist Propaganda, Europol's European Counter Terrorism Centre, The Hague, April 10–11, 2017; Julia Ebner, *The Rage: The Vicious Circle of Islamist and Far-Right Extremism* (London: Tauris, 2017).

9. J. M. Berger, "Making CVE Work: A Focused Approach Based on Process Disruption," *International Centre for Counter-Terrorism—The Hague* 7, no. 5 (2016).

10. Greg Miller and Scott Higham, "In a Propaganda War against ISIS, the U.S. Tried to Play by the Enemy's Rules," *Washington Post*, May 8, 2015.

11. Berger, "Making CVE Work."

12. Spencer Ackerman, "FBI Fired Sebastian Gorka for Anti-Muslim Diatribes," *Daily Beast*, June 21, 2017, https://www.thedailybeast.com/fbi-fired -sebastian-gorka-for-anti-muslim-diatribes; Ayaan Hirsi Ali, "Why the United States Should Back Islam's Reformation," *Dallas Morning News*, August 14, 2015, https://www.belfercenter.org/publication/ayaan-hirsi-ali-why -united-states-should-back-islams-reformation.

13. Hannah Arendt, "Thinking and Moral Considerations: A Lecture," *Social Research* 38, no. 3 (1971): 417–446.

14. This section is adapted from J. M. Berger, "Extremist Construction of Identity: How Escalating Demands for Legitimacy Shape and Define In-Group and Out-Group Dynamics," *International Centre for Counter-Terrorism—The Hague* 8, no. 7 (2017).

15. "President Obama's Remarks at the Islamic Society of Baltimore," *Baltimore Sun*, February 3, 2016, http://www.baltimoresun.com/news/maryland/ bs-md-obama-mosque-visit-remarks-20160203-story.html.

16. For example, "Developing Effective Counter-Narrative Frameworks for Countering Violent Extremism," Meeting Note, International Centre for Counter-Terrorism—The Hague, September 2014, https://www.dhs.gov/sites/ default/files/publications/Developing%20Effective%20Frameworks%20for %20CVE-Hedayah_ICCT%20Report.pdf.

17. Berger, "Extremist Construction of Identity."

18. Akil N. Awan, "Success of the Meta-Narrative: How Jihadists Maintain Legitimacy," *CTC Sentinel* 2, no. 11 (2009): 6–9; William McCants, *The ISIS Apocalypse: The History, Strategy, and Doomsday Vision of the Islamic State* (New York: Macmillan, 2015), 18–20, 37, 79–82.

19. To cite only a few examples: Michael King and Donald M. Taylor, "The Radicalization of Homegrown Jihadists: A Review of Theoretical Models and Social Psychological Evidence," *Terrorism and Political Violence* 23, no. 4 (2011): 602–622; Randy Borum, "Radicalization into Violent Extremism II: A Review of Conceptual Models and Empirical Research," *Journal of Strategic Security* 4, no. 4 (2011): 37; Coyt D. Hargus, "Islamic Radicalization and the Global Islamist Movement: Protecting U.S. National Interests by Understanding and Countering Islamist Grand Strategy with U.S. Policy," Joint Advanced Warfighting School, Joint Forces Staff College, National Defense University, Norfolk, VA, 2013; Peter Neumann and Scott Kleinmann, "How Rigorous Is Radicalization Research?," *Democracy and Security* 9, no. 4 (2013): 360–382; Andrew Hoskins and Ben O'Loughlin, "Media and the Myth of Radicalization," *Media, War, & Conflict* 2, no. 2 (2009): 107–110; Clark McCauley and Sophia

Moskalenko, "Mechanisms of Political Radicalization: Pathways toward Terrorism," *Terrorism and Political Violence* 20, no. 3 (2008): 415–433.

20. Jessica Stern and J. M. Berger, *ISIS: The State of Terror* (New York: HarperCollins, 2015), 25–30, 35–39, ff.

21. Steven Pinker, *The Better Angels of Our Nature: Why Violence Has Declined* (New York: Penguin Books, 2012).

22. Dominic Abrams, "Extremism Is Normal: The Roles of Deviance and Uncertainty in Shaping Groups and Society," in *Extremism and the Psychology of Uncertainty*, ed. Michael A. Hogg and Danielle L. Blaylock, 36–54 (New York: Wiley, 2011).

23. J. M. Berger, "The Awakening," *Foreign Policy*, November 13, 2012, http://foreignpolicy.com/2012/11/13/the-awakening; J. M. Berger, "Fringe Following," *Foreign Policy*, March 28, 2015; http://foreignpolicy.com/2013/03/28/fringe-following; J. M. Berger, "#Unfollow," *Foreign Policy*, February 20, 2013, http://foreignpolicy.com/2013/02/20/unfollow; J. M. Berger, "Following the Money Men," Intelwire, June 14, 2014, http://news.intelwire.com/2014/06/following-money-men.html.

24. John Horgan and Jessica Stern, "Terrorism Research Has Not Stagnated," *Chronicle of Higher Education* 8 (2013).

BIBLIOGRAPHY

This book is an effort to distill several years of research into extremist ideologies and propaganda into a short, accessible text. As such, readers may have more specific questions about how some of these concepts were developed. The readings below provide considerably more detail about the process that led to these conclusions.

On the ideological evolution of British Israelism into Christian Identity and how the identity construction concepts in this book were derived:

Berger, J. M. "Extremist Construction of Identity: How Escalating Demands for Legitimacy Shape and Define In-Group and Out-Group Dynamics." *International Centre for Counter-Terrorism—The Hague* 8, no. 7 (2017). https://icct .nl/publication/extremist-construction-of-identity-how-escalating-demands -for-legitimacy-shape-and-define-in-group-and-out-group-dynamics.

On concepts used in Islamic State propaganda, including additional identity construction elements and crisis-solution constructs:

Berger, J. M. "Countering Islamic State Messaging through 'Linkage-Based' Analysis." *International Centre for Counter-Terrorism—The Hague* 8, no. 2 (2017). https://icct.nl/publication/countering-islamic-state-messaging -through-linkage-based-analysis.

On crisis-solution constructs and systems of meaning:

Ingram, H. J. "The Strategic Logic of the 'Linkage-Based' Approach to Combating Militant Islamist Propaganda: Conceptual and Empirical Foundations." *International Centre for Counter-Terrorism—The Hague* 8, no. 6 (2017). https:// icct.nl/publication/the-strategic-logic-of-the-linkage-based-approach-to -combating-militant-islamist-propaganda-conceptual-and-empirical-foundations.

On uncertainty-identity theory:

Hogg, Michael A., and Danielle Blaylock, eds. *Extremism and the Psychology of Uncertainty*. Malden, MA: Wiley, 2012.

On countering violent extremism, including a review of research related to causes and drivers of extremism and the individual radicalization model:

Berger, J. M. "Making CVE Work: A Focused Approach Based on Process Disruption." *International Centre for Counter-Terrorism—The Hague* 7, no. 5 (2016). https://icct.nl/publication/making-cve-work-a-focused-approach-based-on-process-disruption.

Additional Readings

Berger, J. M. "Tailored Online Interventions: The Islamic State's Recruitment Strategy." *CTC Sentinel* 8, no. 10 (October 2015).

Berger, J. M. "The *Turner* Legacy: The Storied Origins and Enduring Impact of White Nationalism's Deadly Bible." *International Centre for Counter-Terrorism—The Hague* 7, no. 8 (2016). https://icct.nl/publication/the-turner-legacy-the-storied-origins-and-enduring-impact-of-white-nationalisms-deadly-bible.

Cohn, Norman. *The Pursuit of the Millennium: Revolutionary Millenarians and Mystical Anarchists of the Middle Ages*. New York: Oxford University Press, 1970, expanded Kindle edition 2011.

Evans, Richard J. *The Coming of the Third Reich*. New York: Penguin, 2005.

Faust, D. G., ed. *The Ideology of Slavery: Proslavery Thought in the Antebellum South, 1830–1860*. Baton Rouge: Louisiana State University Press, 1981.

Hofstadter, Richard. *The Paranoid Style in American Politics*. New York: Vintage, 2012.

Landes, Richard, and Steven T. Katz. *The Paranoid Apocalypse: A Hundred-Year Retrospective on the Protocols of the Elders of Zion*. New York: New York University Press, 2012.

Léglu, C., R. Rist, and C. Taylor, eds. *The Cathars and the Albigensian Crusade: A Sourcebook*. New York: Routledge, 2013.

Naimark, Norman M. *Genocide: A World History*. New York: Oxford University Press, 2016.

Schmid, Alex P. "The Definition of Terrorism." In *The Routledge Handbook of Terrorism Research*, ed. Alex P. Schmid, 39–157. New York: Routledge, 2011.

Stern, Jessica, and J. M. Berger. *ISIS: The State of Terror*. New York: HarperCollins, 2015.

Tajfel, Henri, M. G. Billig, R. P. Bundy, and Claude Flament. "Social Categorization and Intergroup Behaviour." *European Journal of Social Psychology* 1, no. 2 (1971): 149–178.

Waters, Anita M. "Conspiracy Theories as Ethnosociologies: Explanation and Intention in African American Political Culture." *Journal of Black Studies* 28, no. 1 (1997): 112–125.

Zelin, Aaron. "The Intellectual Origins of al-Qaeda's Ideology: The Abolishment of the Caliphate through the Afghan Jihad, 1924–1989." Master's thesis, Brandeis University, 2010.

FURTHER READING

Books

Barkun, Michael. *Religion and the Racist Right: The Origins of the Christian Identity Movement*. Chapel Hill: University of North Carolina Press Books, 1997.

Hogg, Michael A., and Danielle Blaylock, eds. *Extremism and the Psychology of Uncertainty*. Malden, MA: Wiley, 2012.

Landes, R., and S. T. Katz, eds. *The Paranoid Apocalypse: A Hundred-Year Retrospective on the Protocols of the Elders of Zion*. New York: NYU Press, 2012.

McCants, William. *The ISIS Apocalypse: The History, Strategy, and Doomsday Vision of the Islamic State*. New York: Macmillan, 2015.

Naimark, Norman M. *Genocide: A World History*. New York: Oxford University Press, 2016.

Stern, Jessica. *Terror in the Name of God: Why Religious Militants Kill*. New York: Ecco, 2004.

Papers

Available free at https://icct.nl/topic/counter-terrorism-strategic-communications-ctsc.

Berger, J. M. "Extremist Construction of Identity: How Escalating Demands for Legitimacy Shape and Define In-Group and Out-Group Dynamics." *International Centre for Counter-Terrorism—The Hague* 8, no. 7 (2017).

Berger, J. M. "Making CVE Work: A Focused Approach Based on Process Disruption." *International Centre for Counter-Terrorism—The Hague* 7, no. 5 (2016).

Ingram, H. J. "A Brief History of Propaganda during Conflict: Lessons for Counter-Terrorism Strategic Communications." *International Centre for Counter-Terrorism—The Hague* 7, no. 6 (2016).

Ingram, H. J. "The Strategic Logic of the 'Linkage-Based' Approach to Combating Militant Islamist Propaganda: Conceptual and Empirical Foundations." *International Centre for Counter-Terrorism—The Hague* 8, no. 6 (2017).

Reed, Alastair, H. J. Ingram, and Joe Whittaker. "Countering Terrorist Narratives." European Parliament Policy Department for Citizens' Rights and Constitutional Affairs. November 2017.

INDEX

J. M. BERGER is the author of *Jihad Joe: Americans Who Go to War in the Name of Islam* and coauthor (with Jessica Stern) of *ISIS: The State of Terror*. He is a Research Fellow with the VOX-Pol Network of Excellence and a nonresident fellow with the Alliance for Securing Democracy.